Boys and Girls
at Worship

Boys and Girls at Worship

By

MARIE COLE POWELL

PUBLISHERS

HARPER & BROTHERS

NEW YORK *and* LONDON

This Book is Dedicated
with Deep Appreciation
to
WARREN THOMSON POWELL

CONTENTS

INTRODUCTION

Dr. Boynton Merrill tells the story of entering his church one weekday morning and finding a twelve-year-old boy sitting near one of the pillars in the nave of the church. The boy asked,

"Do you mind if I sit here?"

"Of course not," replied the minister.

Then the boy said, "This is a very beautiful church, isn't it?"

"Why, I think it is," said Dr. Merrill.

"It does things to you," the boy went on.

"What does it do to you?" asked Dr. Merrill.

"Well," said the boy, "it makes you all kind of quiet inside and it makes you feel bigger than you are."

In the world in which we live today there is need for some experience which will make it possible for us to "feel all quiet inside and bigger than we are." We shall never be able to face life unless there is some central core of quiet within ourselves to which we can retreat for strength and energy to live in this bewildering world.

Furthermore, it is necessary only to point out that this world of today has made many of us feel very insignificant indeed. Our faith in the innate goodness of man is challenged as never before. So much that was on the way to being good has been torn down and destroyed, not only in the world of material things, but in the human spirit itself, that we are tempted to yield to a sense of futility and personal inadequacy. Surely, we need some experience that will raise us from the dust, that will assure us that we "are bigger than we are," that will show us there is a force forever and unshakably good at the heart of the universe with which we can and must ally ourselves. For some of us that experience without which we cannot live is the experience of worship.

And let us not think for one moment that this is entirely an adult problem. We are indeed, impoverished spiritually if we must stand helpless before the questioning faces of our boys and girls; if, when they ask us for a loaf, we can hand them only a stone. They will sense in us our uncertainty; they have already caught the note of despair, some of them, from the adults whom they know.

A sense of adequacy and power may come in several ways, and each of these ways may be greatly enriched by that experience which we call worship. In the first place, every child needs to be able to interpret his experience. To understand it, to see meanings that underlie it—this supplies that zest for living which Dr. Coe says is an essential aspect of genuine worship. "Seeing what underlies" is becoming increasingly difficult for adults living in the hurried complexity of the present age, which, of course, means that it will be difficult for the children of these adults. Moments of quiet withdrawal from the scene of action are absolutely essential if bewilderment is to give place to a sense of purpose and if a superficial speeding over the surface of life is to be halted now and then by prolonged glimpses into the possible depths of experience.

Boys and girls between the ages of nine and fourteen are not naturally introspective, and it is not the purpose of worship to make them so. But there is nothing alien to the natural approach of childhood in the habit of quiet thinking and feeling about people, events and the great universe of which they are a part. Life for them now and in the future years can take on the quality of an adventurous quest if they begin, while they are still young, to discover that it has meaning and purpose.

A second path to religious living is a sustained belief in the abiding values of beauty, goodness and truth. In worship some of these values, which may appear to be threatened, are celebrated so that, with the assurance that now abideth faith, hope and love, we may go out from moments of worship, even as did such mystics as St. Francis and John Woolman, to live lives in which a little more of goodness and truth and beauty shall enrich the world.

A third path to spiritual power lies in the direction of religious experience which is absolutely sincere and real. To guide boys and girls through worship experiences that shall be genuine requires that adult leaders understand what are real religious experiences to children.

As one thinks about some of the people who have lived rich, full lives, it becomes apparent that time and place do not necessarily determine the quality of experience. Rose Cristopher, a high-school girl, sensed this fact when she wrote,

> Some people say experience is travel,
> Seeing
> Strange, bizarre, exotic places;
>
> .   .   .   .   .
>
> And yet I say experience
> Is merely our ability to endow ordinary
>   people and ordinary places
> With unordinary
> Meanings.[1]

One of the characteristics of religion has been its ability to suggest the "unordinary" meanings that lie at the heart of everyday experience.

Children accept this aspect of experience as a thing to be expected. They do not, of their own accord, separate the so-called "religious" from the secular aspects of experience. Any experience, for them, holds within itself the possibilities of religious interpretation. They, like the poets, who at heart are always children, find it easy to believe that

> Here on the paths of every day—
> Here on the common human way
> Is all the stuff the gods would take
> To build a Heaven.[2]

It is well for us who have the guidance of children to remind ourselves often that, though we label certain experiences as "religious" and complacently assume that children are having a religious experience, actually the boys and girls may not be acquiring any religious

[1] From "Experience," in *Younger Poets*, Nellie B. Sergent, Ed., D. Appleton-Century Company, 1932.

[2] From "Earth Is Enough," by Edwin Markham, in *The Shoes of Happiness and Other Poems,* Doubleday, Doran & Co., 1913, page 115. Used by permission of Mr. Virgil Markham.

values. On the other hand, they may be experiencing life on a very deep religious level through some activities which do not bear the tag "religious."

We sometimes refer to going to church as a "specifically religious activity"; yet, how many children have wiggled in the family pew, have drawn pictures and have gone home tired and hungry to their Sunday dinners without having experienced anything which could even remotely be called religious. On the other hand, everyday life, in many other situations than that of churchgoing, holds countless opportunities for making boys and girls, as well as adults, "feel bigger than they are."

We have already noted that there are plenty of factors in our complex modern civilization to make children feel smaller than they are and utterly unable to cope with situations. It requires the wise guidance of fathers and mothers and teachers to help the boys and girls of today to grow up feeling equal to the tasks of life, "to feel bigger than they are." The first clause of the White House Charter for Childhood states: "For every child spiritual and moral training to help him stand firm under the pressure of life." We may be offering the child a carefully organized curriculum of religious education in the church; we may be putting him through certain religious exercises in the home; we may even be inviting him Sunday after Sunday to participate in carefully planned services of worship; and we think that we are girding him with strength to "stand firm under the pressure of life." But if at the same time we are so unaware of his psychological needs that we are developing in him a sense of inferiority, if we are giving him a concept of religion which makes him always dependent *upon* God rather than a strong, independent *worker with God*, the experience which we offer him may lack the quality of genuine up-building religion.

At the heart of religion lies the experience of fellowship with One other than and greater than ourselves. What ever experiences will open the child's eyes to the wonder and the beauty of the world will prepare him for fellowship with the Creator of this wonder and beauty. Whatever experiences give him a sense of security and a feeling of the dependability of the universe will strengthen his belief in God. When he meets in those who guide him, in home and school, kindness, belief in others, friendliness with all races and classes, nobility of ethical action, composure in all the vicissitudes of life, he is gradually forming a concept of a God who is kindness, mercy and goodness and of a religion that has sources of power. If he early feels himself a member of a group that shares creative endeavors for making home and the larger world outside the home a happy place for all people, then he is prepared to enter into that fullness of religious experience which comes through a sense of being a creative co-operator with God.

One of the greatest needs of the day in which we live is that people shall discover that genuine satisfaction of human longing which may come through the practice of worship. A life habit of establishing communication with the Eternal Spirit is more likely to be built up by beginning with *boys* and *girls* and by attempting to lead them into religious experiencing that to *them* is emotionally and intellectually satisfying.

The experience of worship may occur in a variety of situations and may be induced by different types of stimuli. For all children of any age there is a reality in worship that occurs in the midst of experience as over against that which is a celebration of life after the experience has become a thing of the past. This is one reason why religious educators are emphasizing the necessity for boys and girls of some worship that is informal and that grows out of the activities challenging their interest.

Worship of this kind requires careful planning. If our departments are made up of three grades, with several classes to a grade, how can we provide for this departmental group some common activities for all the classes so that real experiences of worship can be shared by all? There can be some departmental activities as well as class enterprises, or some way in which class projects can contribute to some major departmental enterprise and the class experiences be shared with the entire group. In schools with a limited time schedule it might be well to shorten the period allotted to worship occasionally and use this time for a departmental assembly, which would actually be building up a group experience so meaningful that when the group was "ready" for worship, there would be no doubt about the reality of the experience.

One of the basic needs of boys and girls is for sufficient variety to hold attention and to invest worship services with vividness of appeal. Pearcy Dearmer says, "Again let me insist on what the psychologist knows so well, that variation lies at the heart of attention and therefore of all fervor in worship."[3] Mr. Dearmer is speaking of adult worshipers, but his statement is even more true of boys and girls.

Variety of environment may be one means of stimulating the mood of worship. Boys and girls between the ages of nine and fourteen are mature enough to worship in a churchly environment, either in a beautiful chapel enriched with the symbols of worship or in a church-school room which has been made worshipful by the introduction of an altar on which are candles and a bowl of flowers, with a soft curtain of some rich color behind the altar and an appropriate picture occasionally hanging against this background over the altar. Often the church sanctuary itself is too large for a small group, but in small churches, it may provide an inspiring environment for worship by small groups.

On the other hand, boys and girls of this age often feel a certain reality in the worship experience when it occurs in a less formal, more intimate setting. There is a beautiful chapel in the Grand Teton Mountains which, in place of a painted altar piece or a silk curtain, has over the altar a great window which frames a view of the snow peaks. For a group of boys and girls to arrive some Sunday morning to find that the chairs for the worship services have been changed to face the windows through which they glimpse a gray sky and a mass of soft, whirling snowflakes; to see on a low table before the windows a vase

[3] Percy Dearmer, *The Art of Public Worship*, Morehouse Gorham Company, 1919, page 103.

holding a single, beautiful rose and then to read some poetry about snow and to sing the following hymn— this may give worship a freshness and vitality which it might lack in the more formal setting.

> All beautiful the march of days,
>> As seasons come and go;
> The hand that shaped the rose hath wrought
>> The crystal of the snow;
> Hath sent the hoary frost of heaven,
>> The flowing waters sealed,
> And laid a silent loveliness
>> On hill and wood and field.[4]

Boys and girls of this age respond to the homelike intimacy of a group seated before an open fire. Or, they may feel a sudden hush fall upon their spirits around the campfire in the open air with sentinel pines keeping watch and overhead the distant stars. In such a setting, "Lord of the sunlight, Lord of the starlight" may take on a significance it never could have if sung a week later in a more churchly environment. Let us, in planning the worship experiences of boys and girls, remember that they are eager for sensory experience, that they crave some elements of spontaneity in their worship and that certain intimate, informal environments may provide for an expression of worship feelings which emerge out of immediate experiences.

As boys and girls grow older we are apt to assume that they are ready for and need only a formal service of worship in a formal setting. But if we had more

[4] Frances W. Wile, "All beautiful the march of days," *Beacon Song and Service Book*, No. 222, Beacon Press, 1935.

adequate ways of evaluating the outcome of so intangible an experience as worship, we should probably discover that their buoyant spirits, their zest for life, their need to bring order out of the confusion of experiences which life brings to the modern child demand some type of informal group meeting as well as the more formal services of worship.

This book has attempted to give suggestions for both types of worship experiences, the formal and informal. Since any individual of any age receives the most benefit from worship if he is aware of its purposes, if he understands and appreciates the materials through which he is worshiping, if the desire to worship and a feeling of expectancy are stimulated and if there is a strong sense of fellowship in the worshiping group, this book includes some suggestions for worship of an informal type as well as for more formal services. Sometimes the less formal approach precedes, sometimes it follows the formal experience.

"The wind bloweth where it listeth" and the spirit of man establishes sudden connections with the Spirit of God, under the skillful guidance of such informal periods of group fellowship. The leader of worship should be sensitive to this mood of reverence, wonder or happiness and at times be prepared swiftly to provide expression for it in a brief prayer, a moment of silence or the singing of a hymn, even though these were not in the original plan.

The question of pupil leadership of worship services is one that needs thoughtful consideration. Increasingly during the years between nine and fifteen, boys and girls are capable of real leadership in all school enterprises. Let us be sure that all pupil leadership of worship is a growth that comes from *within* and not a task superimposed from *without*. Such leadership is valuable when it develops from a sharing process in which, in informal assembly or class periods, pupils suggest themes for worship, occasionally search for appropriate materials or plan certain services of worship for definite occasions. Sometimes this leadership involves real creative endeavor in which individuals, small groups or the entire group create their own materials of worship.

On certain occasions pupils may participate in the leadership of worship by taking the place of the adult leader, by reading scripture or poetry, by telling stories or by interpreting to the group certain class experiences. If pupils are to participate in such leadership of worship it should be easy and natural. Self-conscious children should not be pushed into a performance as difficult for them as it will be unpleasant to the other worshipers. In church schools in which democracy *is* a way of life and pupil participation in *all* of the school activities is the usual thing, leadership in worship takes its place along with other types of leadership as a natural activity.

However, there are a few cautions to be kept in mind. The function of all such leadership is to sustain the worship mood in the worshiping group. As far as possible *all* should be worshiping *all* the time. So, poor readers should not be allowed to inhibit the appreciation of the selection to be read. Pupil musicians should not be asked to render poor performances merely for the sake of giving them an opportunity to participate. If a pupil is to read, let him be a good reader and let the standard of careful preparation for each type of participation be strictly adhered to. If there are pupils with unusual musical ability let them occasionally realize the joy of interpreting some part of the worship service through their music.

But above everything else, let us remember that to guide an experience of worship is a highly developed art which demands the mature skill of an adult. Under trained adult guidance children may feel that they are participating freely and democratically in a service of worship to which they have made creative contributions, even though an adult, and not a child, does the actual leading. But, since we are seeking to maintain balance in our program building, let us make a place for those occasional services through which the boys and girls share some meaningful experience with others in the group or some group invited in to worship with them.

In planning a program of worship for any group in the church school, we are confronted with such questions as the following: What are the interests and needs of this particular group to which worship can and should minister? Some of these interests and needs are distinctly personal; others lie in the social areas of this group's expanding world. How can I, as a leader, keep a balance between the personal and the social emphasis in the worship services? Are there other balances which I ought to keep in mind, such as that between formal and informal worship experiences, between adult and pupil leadership, between worship that brings challenging problems into our communion with God and that which provides for the expression of great moods of appreciation? What experiences are most real to this group and how can the experience of worship be related to these other realities? And, last of all, how can I, as a leader, become more creative in my worship planning so that I need to lean less and less on printed worship guides and can venture to explore the great field of worship literature and gradually become skillful in the art of planning and leading worship?

The worship services in this book are grouped together under certain areas in which some of the real experiencing of boys and girls seems to lie. Home life, play life and broader community and world relationships are given meaning and related to the child's consciousness of God and of his partnership with God in creative living. There are many significant areas which this book does not attempt to cover. Many of the worship themes are capable of expansion over a much longer period of time than that allotted to them in the book. For that reason suggestions are made for further enrichment materials which can be used by the creative leader in planning his own services.

The leader of worship is urged not to feel bound to follow the order in which the themes occur in the book. On the other hand, let him study his own group and select such themes as seem to relate most closely to their immediate interests.

Under each theme some services of worship are worked out in detail. For others in the same series worship materials are offered and only a few suggestions are given. It is hoped that leaders of worship will become more and more able to plan their own services.

Group worship will become real to the extent that the leader shares with the teachers in the group the task of planning worship. Teachers and worship leader should sit down together and talk about the needs of all the children in the group. Teachers will often discover child interests and needs which are not known to the leader of worship. It is as true in worship as in other educational processes that democracy, not autocracy, has within it life-giving qualities. Dr. Bode in his book, *Democracy as a Way of Life*, says, "To have life and to have it more abundantly becomes a matter...of continuous growth in the capacity to lift this principle of common interests and purposes out of its various and ever-changing contexts and to make it the basis of a consistent way of life."[5] All of the children's workers in a group working together for all of the children—this is the way of democracy that may lead to abundant life.

In this matter of making worship real, it is evident that the class teacher has a unique opportunity. The realization of the presence of God is not dependent upon a formal service of worship, but comes often when small groups are working together upon a challenging task. If the teacher realizes that she, too, may guide her class sessions so that boys and girls will feel like worshiping, then, it makes possible a worship

[5] Boyd Bode, *Democracy as a Way of Life*, The Macmillan Company, 1937, page 52.

experience which may result when study and activity are immediately related to worship.

When we begin to think deeply about worship we realize how closely integrated it is, or may be, with the entire program of religious education. The capacity to enter into the fullness of the worship experience depends, in part, upon the religious level on which an individual lives. The more completely we share God's purposes and the more nearly we live each day as a child of God the more genuine will be our communion with Him.

It follows, then, that when we are helping children to grow in character, to substitute consideration for others for self-interest, to make right decisions in the realm of conduct and to build up wholesome and desirable habits, just so far are we making it possible for them with genuine sincerity to pray,

> Help us to do the things we should,
> To be to others kind and good.

If we teach children to pray for such help from God and then leave them unprotected by guidance in how to help that prayer come true, are we not in danger of encouraging worship that is insincere and unreal? We are coming more and more to see that religious education cannot be mass education. Individual guidance of children must mean something more than an occasional visit into the child's home, a hurried consultation with the parents or a spasmodic conversation with the child himself. It involves careful and painstaking records of the growth of the child, meeting him individually and in a group far oftener than one hour a

week and equipping ourselves with all the skills possible to foster individual growth.

It would be ideal if all our worship services could
grow out of the actual experiencing of the group. This
is possible only when the church-school program is of a
highly integrated character, where all in the worshiping
group are engaged in the same curriculum activity. In
most church schools at present any departmental worship is participated in by classes, each following a
different curriculum unit. To relate worship to these
various interests is a very difficult task.

For this reason, there are listed a few activities in
which the entire worshiping group may participate—
activities which could be closely related to the worship
experiences. Each leader will have to decide how practical it is in his particular church situation to carry out
these activities. Some of them could be suggested as
home projects, if there is no opportunity for carrying
them out in the group work in the church school. Some
can be carried out as class enterprises and discussed
in the larger group in assembly periods preceding the
services of worship.

There is a very real danger that an individual's
interest in religion may remain always on the purely
personal level. Man was made to grow, in his religious
as in other experiences. To be able to live richly and
fully in the lives of others is one mark of maturity.
Boys and girls need, as they are passing through the
pre-adolescent years, to begin to learn to lose themselves in some experiences which, while they are in
many respects close enough to their everyday world to
challenge genuine interest, yet may lift them out of a

self-centered existence into a larger fellowship which includes workers and worshipers of the past and of the present.

It is for these reasons that the worship services in this book begin with an interest which is native to the years between nine and fourteen and then expand that interest to larger dimensions. When we bring the matter of "our friends" into the realm of worship, we do not leave it on the narrow, personal plane, but expand the concept to include the fellowship of the church.

Beginning with the rich sensory experience which boys and girls crave, we glimpse how essential beauty has been and is to men and women and how the creation of beauty for the enrichment of the life of the world has related the creators to the creative processes of God.

Boys and girls of this age know, from their own firsthand experiences in the field of leisure-time activity, what it is to lose one's self in a project that challenges all one's wholehearted interest. Therefore, they can be led into an appreciation of what it means to the workers of the world to be given a chance to do their work under conditions that release instead of imprison them.

Christmas, an experience so dear to the heart of every boy and girl, may be purely selfish and superficial in its implications. Or, it may be lifted to a higher level—a level where genuine religious values prevail.

Even our dreams and our hopes, which are often so entirely self-centered, at moments are shot through with gleams from a more universal and immortal atmosphere. Why not, in moments of worship, examine these dreams and lift them to that realm where they are consciously related to "God's dreams"?

It will be noted that these services of worship emphasize such fundamental and abiding experiences as aspiration, beauty, work, friendship. Long ago Dr. Cabot selected four major life-needs as those by which men live—work, play, love and worship.[6] A recent educator lists the enthusiasms by which men live as man's enthusiasm for his work, for his play, for his personal relationships and for his religion.[7] In spite of a world tottering on the brink of disaster—rather, *because* of it—men must hold on to some of these values which abide forever. To realize that one can and must create beauty in a world where beauty is being crushed to earth; to see in one's work the opportunity to build for others while we fellowship with God; to realize that that social instinct which prompts us to reach out to others may be a life-creating force which each one of us may consciously set loose in the world, that we may "dream from our despair democracy"—these are some of the realizations which, in terms of boy and girl comprehension, the following services of worship seek to achieve. If the boys and girls glimpse some of these things as they participate in worship experiences month after month; if, by so doing, they are establishing the habit of securing for themselves moments of quiet and worshipful thinking; if they gradually come to

[6] See Richard Cabot, *What Men Live By,* Houghton Mifflin Company, 1914.

[7] "Four Enthusiasms Men Live By" by Linwood Chase, in the *Christian Register.*

enjoy the "collected sanctuary of the spirit" which group worship affords—then, perhaps, we are setting them on their way with something to hold to in years of suffering or of happiness.

1

DREAMS

"Dreams are they—but they are God's dreams!"

All children, at one time or another, indulge in dreaming of the future. Although junior boys and girls cannot be said to be thinking seriously of specific vocations, yet their imagination is of the practical kind which invents plans the children then try to carry out. Watch any neighborhood group at their play and note how they will act out dramatically the play which they have planned and how they will sustain their interest in this purposeful play from day to day, sometimes over a period of several weeks. This type of imagination is that used by all inventors, scientists and social reformers—those who build a practical dream whose fulfillment might benefit mankind. Since boys and girls between the ages of eight and twelve respond alertly to experiences which stimulate this practical imagination, why not help them to dream dreams of accomplishment which will include the welfare of all mankind?

Lest someone should object that we are encouraging boys and girls to indulge in wishful thinking, as a substitute for action, let us remember that wishful thinking need not remain on the level of a mere wish, and that it is a peculiarly common quality of children

I

of this age to want to work out their dreams in some practical and tangible form. The social-service activities of the church school should, therefore, be emphasized during this series of services of worship, so that while the children are having experiences of dreaming they are at the same time working actively to embody these dreams of social welfare in plans of action.

It is a high privilege to lead a group of boys and girls in an experience of worship. It demands of the leader a sincere commitment to those values which he seeks to make real and challenging to the worshiping group.

Before embarking upon the worship programs suggested in the following pages, it would be well to read all the material suggested on the subject of dreams and to become thoroughly saturated with the spirit of these services. The following poem mentions some of the dreams which we, as adults, may share with God and with the children. Let us read in the spirit of worship and ask ourselves

"Can we say nay as they claim us?"

God's Dreams

Dreams are they—but they are God's dreams!
Shall we deny them and scorn them?
That men shall love one another,
That white shall call black man brother,
That greed shall pass from the market place,
That lust shall yield to love for their race,
That man shall meet with God face to face—
Dreams are they all,
But shall we despise them—
God's Dreams!

Dreams are they—to become man's dreams!
Can we say nay as they claim us?
That men shall cease from their hating,
That war shall soon be abating,
That the glory of kings and lords shall pale,
That the pride of dominion and power shall fail,
That the love of humanity shall prevail—
Dreams are they all,
But shall we despise them—
God's Dreams.[1]

SERVICES OF WORSHIP

FIRST SERVICE OF WORSHIP

If the following services are to be used at the beginning of the school year, it might be well to sing the familiar hymn, "O Beautiful for Spacious Skies," as an introduction to the series and as a means of creating a spirit of fellowship and of associating the content of the hymn with the children's summer vacations. Sing the first verse and then pause for informal conversation about the summer experiences just past. Such questions as the following may stimulate responses from the group:

LEADER: We are singing one of the best-loved hymns about our own country. We have just returned from our summer vacations. I wonder how many of you spent them in any parts of America described in the hymn.

RESPONSES FROM GROUP:

LEADER: There are some vacation spots in America not mentioned in our hymn. Perhaps some of you were in those places.

[1] By Thomas Curtis Clark in *One Thousand Quotable Poems*, Willett, Clark & Company, 1931.

RESPONSES: Seashore, cities, villages.

LEADER: If some of you spent your vacations in the city, you probably discovered some delightful vacation spots right at home.

POSSIBLE RESPONSES: City parks, public beaches, playgrounds, etc.

LEADER: In the other verses of the hymn a new thought is given. They suggest that perhaps America is not perfect. As we sing, shall we think of ways in which America might be better?

After singing the remaining verses of the hymn, the leader might ask if, during their vacations, the boys and girls saw any "flaws" that needed to be mended. Or any unhappiness. Call attention to the lines,

> O beautiful for patriot dream
> That sees beyond the years
> Thine alabaster cities gleam
> Undimm'd by human tears![2]

What kind of city does the writer imagine when she talks of "alabaster cities gleaming"? Let the leader explain how the writer dreams of beautiful homes of marble glistening in the sunshine. What are the happenings that bring "human tears" to dim the beauty of our cities?

Members of the group may mention crowded sections of cities, inadequate playgrounds, child labor, conditions in mining sections, migrant labor. Some may mention moving pictures, like "Grapes of Wrath." It is well to be prepared to help boys and girls to gain a true understanding of the implications of such pictures, so that

[2] From "America the Beautiful," by Katharine Lee Bates.

they may separate from the exciting action the real causes of sorrow and suffering.

LEADER: Our hymn speaks of

> ....heroes proved,
> In liberating strife,
> Who more than self their country loved,
> And mercy more than life.

Do any such heroes come to your mind who have helped to make any of these unhappy conditions better? RESPONSES: (Be prepared for a variety of responses. The leader may want to add to the list, suggesting such names as Jane Addams, Muriel Lester and other present-day leaders who are helping to make a world "undimm'd by human tears.")
LEADER: It is easy to see, isn't it, that if we are to have a happier world, some people must first dream a dream of how to make it better? I am going to tell you an old story of a boy who once dreamed such a dream.

Story. "Behold! This Dreamer!"[3]

Once upon a time, a great many years ago, in a little Oriental village there lived a carpenter. This carpenter and his wife had a large family of children, but the work was made easy for them because of the oldest boy in the family. This son helped his father in the carpenter's shop; he played with the younger children and took them on long tramps up in the hills to pick bunches of red lilies and many times he helped his

[3] Used by permission of the Board of Education, Methodist Church.

mother sweep out their plain little house or fetch water from the village well.

Now the carpenter noticed that though his oldest son was a good worker, he was also a dreamer. Sometimes, when work was over, he sat with a far-away look in his eyes, as though he were thinking up some plan. The carpenter would have been surprised had he known that sometimes his boy was thinking about him. For the boy had noticed some things about his father.

It happened that, at the time of this story, the country was under the rule of a foreign power and there were foreign soldiers in many of the towns and villages. Sometimes these soldiers would clank up and down the village streets looking very proud and insolent and the boy's blood would rush to his cheeks and his fist would start to clench in anger. His father, the carpenter, would notice it and say in a quiet way, "Wait a minute, my son, where will it get you if you strike out in passionate anger? Remember, a soft answer turneth away wrath."

Over and over again the boy saw his father, even when the soldiers were insolent to him, remain courteous and gentle; over and over again when the younger brothers and sisters were quarrelsome or neglected their duties, the boy watched the carpenter, his father, and saw how his kindness to them and his love for them never changed.

So, when he sat with the far-away look in his eyes he was dreaming a great dream—What if God was like his father! In some of the old stories of his people, back in the days when they had lived in the midst of danger on the desert, their law had been "an eye for an eye and a tooth for a tooth," until they had sometimes thought of God as an angry God. But, one of their prophets had said that God was a loving, forgiving God. Yes, what if God was like his father, the carpenter!

Now, the boy's dream had two other parts to it. First, if God was like a loving father, perhaps his children could be always loving too. The boy's own father, the carpenter, was. What if a boy like himself could not clench his fists in anger but be always loving and forgiving? Why not try? No one must know. This was his secret dream. But he would practice and see.

How hard it was to smile pleasantly at the Roman soldier who pushed him out of the way! But, he managed it. It was not easy, when his younger brother James mislaid his favorite carpenter's tool, but he managed to forgive him and be gentle and James brought it back again. When he tried to tell them some of the things he was dreaming about and they laughed at him, it was hard not to get angry or to feel hurt. But, somehow, he felt more and more sure that his new dream was a true one—that if you loved people hard enough they would become more kind themselves. Sometimes, it didn't seem to work, but he kept on believing and dreaming just the same.

Then, there was the last part of his dream. If God was loving like his own father, if all people could become loving like God, somebody must remind them of this. People didn't realize it, or they kept forgetting.

Was he the one to do it? Would they laugh at him if he tried to tell them? First he must keep on practicing this law of love right in his home and in the village, so when he began to tell them about it they would know he had tried it first himself.

Years passed by and one morning the son of the carpenter left the carpenter shop and walked down the village street to go to other villages in the country to tell his dreams to all people. After he had gone the old friends and neighbors in his own village heard rumors about him from time to time, about how the people were crowding around him to hear what he said.

"Your God is a loving God," he told them. "He sends rain on the just and the unjust too. He is like a loving father, who gives good gifts to his children. And he expects you to be perfect in love, even as he is. He wants you to forgive all your wrongs. He wants you to bring gifts of happiness to others."

Some who heard him said, "He talks as one having authority; as though he had tried these things first himself."

One Sunday morning the old friends and neighbors were surprised when they went to the synagogue to find him there. He was invited to read the scripture and as he rose to read they all listened breathlessly to see what he would choose. And the son of the carpenter chose some verses from the Old Testament which seemed to him to describe his dream. Now—the time was here to let his old friends know what he had been dreaming about all those years. He began to read—

The Spirit of the Lord is upon me,
Because he hath anointed me to preach the gospel to
    the poor;
He hath sent me to heal the broken hearted,
To preach deliverance to the captives and recovering
    of sight to the blind,
To set at liberty them that are bruised.

In the silence that followed, some of them said,
"Is this not Jesus, the son of Joseph, the carpenter?"

The years passed by. When he was finally con-
demned to die on the cross, in the midst of all his
disappointment, he still dreamed that it is better to love
and to forgive than to hate and he said this prayer to
God, "Father, forgive them, for they know not what
they do."

Now, it just happened that a Roman soldier stood
near the cross and heard this prayer. Could it have
been one of those very soldiers who used to push him
out of the way in the little streets of Nazareth? We
do not know, but when this soldier heard the son of the
carpenter, living out his dream to be loving and forgiving in the midst of all that cruelty, the soldier cried
out, "Surely this is a righteous man!"

LEADER: There were other people who felt as the
soldier did. One day after Jesus had been preaching to
the people, some of them said, "He teaches as one
having authority." I think they felt that he had been
practicing some of these laws of love in the quiet
little village of Nazareth before he asked other people
to practice them. One day when a great crowd of people
had come out to hear him on the hillside, he said:

Blessed are ye poor.

Blessed are ye that hunger.

Blessed are ye when men persecute you.

Ye are the salt of the earth.

Ye are the light of the world.

Ye shall be sons of the Most High: for he is kind toward the unthankful and evil: he maketh his sun to rise on the evil and the good, and sendeth rain on the just and the unjust. Be ye merciful, even as your Father is merciful.

Blessed are the merciful: for they shall obtain mercy.[4]

Hymn.   "Praise to the Brave, the True" (To the tune "Dundee")

Praise to the brave, the true, the great,
Who made us what we are!
Who lit the flame which yet shall glow
With radiance brighter far:

Glory to them in coming time—
Thro' ages yet to be:
Who burst Opression's galling chain
And bade the world go free![5]

SECOND SERVICE OF WORSHIP

Let the leader by way of preparation for this service bring out the fact that many boys and girls have had secret daydreams of things they would like to do some day to make this world happier. Sometimes we cannot decide definitely when we are very young what we are going to do, but we can begin to think about all the many ways in which we can help.

[4] From *Jesus As Teacher*, by Henry B. Sharman, Harper & Brothers, 1935, pages 34 and 36.

[5] By Robert Nicoll, in *Beacon Song and Service Book*, Beacon Press, 1935, No. 117.

Suggested approach: One evening Betty, who was eleven years old, didn't go to sleep the minute her head touched the pillow, as she usually did. Her mother heard her moving in her bed and went in to ask what was the matter.

"Oh, I was just dreaming," said Betty.

"But you haven't been asleep, have you?" asked her mother.

"No," said Betty. "I've been dreaming, wideawake, of something I'd like to do sometime."

Her mother wondered if Betty were dreaming of a picnic, or a visit to her grandmother's. She was surprised when Betty said, "I was dreaming that some day I might have a home filled with cunning little Negro babies, little Negro babies who had no fathers and mothers to look after them. Wouldn't it be fun?"

All boys and girls dream, sometimes, of things like this that they would like to do to make people happier. Perhaps, our services of worship will give us some things to dream about which we have not thought of before

Opening Prelude

Call To Worship (Read in unison from the blackboard or mimeographed sheets, if possible)

> We thank thee, Lord, for eyes to see
> The beauty of the earth,
> For ears to hear the words of love
> And happy sounds of mirth.
>
> O, may our eyes be open, Lord,
> To see our neighbor's need,

And may our ears be kept alert
Their cries for help to heed.[6]

Hymn. "The Fathers Built This City"

Story. "How Jane Addams' Dream Came True"

Once upon a time there was a little girl named Jane who lived in a big house in a little town. When she was nearly seven years old, her father took her with him to the big town some miles away where he had an errand to do on a narrow dirty street. There Jane saw two long rows of little houses crowded together on the edge of the street, with no yards in front where the children could play. Jane thought, "This must be what it means to be poor." Then and there she made up her mind what she wanted to do some day. She said to her father, "When I grow up, I am going to have a big house like the one we live in, but it will not be built alongside other big houses, but next to horrid little houses like these."

But many years went by before Jane's dream came true. She went home with her father that day to live with her brothers and sisters in their own big house. She and her favorite brother, George, often played together in the yard under the tall trees. They used to wander over the hills and the woods and the cliffs, and along the creek. There was one cave they especially liked to explore, where they had to light candles to see their way through the dark. Another of their favorite play places was their father's flour mill,

---

[6] Jeanette E. Perkins, *Children's Worship in the Church School*, Harper & Brothers, 1939, page 182.

where they liked to watch the water wheel go round and round. In the basement were piles of bran which the miller would sometimes let them sprinkle with water and make into mountains and walls and towers. It was great fun.

Now during these years while she was growing up Jane almost forgot that in other parts of the world there were children who had no places where they could play except in the crowded and hard streets, and that many boys and girls had to work all day in factories so that they had few opportunities even to play in the streets.

Finally, Jane Addams grew up and left home to go to college. After she was graduated, she went with some friends on a trip to Europe. There they visited old cities and churches and art museums and beautiful countrysides, but always Jane wanted to see how ordinary people lived in these countries. It was in the great city of London, as she was riding on a bus through the poorest section of the city, that she saw people who were really hungry. It was on a Saturday night and Jane Addams was taken, along with a number of other tourists, to see an auction sale where men were auctioning off their unsold vegetables that would not keep until Monday morning. She saw thousands of hands stretched out and up in the air as they grabbed for the rotten vegetables that were really not fit for any one to eat. Miss Addams saw one poor man bid his pennies on a cabbage and then sit right down and gnaw at it without even waiting to clean it or to cook it. And at that moment Jane Addams decided that somehow she must do something about such things.

When she arrived in a certain city in Germany, she saw from the window of her hotel one snowy morning a long file of women with large wooden tanks fastened to their backs. In these tanks they were carrying a hot brew used in making beer. Miss Addams wrote, "The women were bent forward, not only under the weight which they were bearing, but because the tanks were so high that it would have been impossible for them to have lifted their heads. Their faces and hands, reddened in the cold morning air, showed clearly the white scars where they had previously been scalded by the hot stuff which splashed if they stumbled ever so little on their way."

Miss Addams was so horrified that she went at once to the owner of the brewery to ask that something be done to make this work safer for the women, but he merely shrugged his shoulders. That morning Jane Addams could not eat her breakfast. And the dream of what she ought to do to make working conditions better for women and children began to grow clearer.

As Jane Addams continued to travel through Europe, she saw common people everywhere going into the art museums and the beautiful cathedrals. She watched them sitting beside large looms in their homes, weaving cloth in lovely patterns, or making pottery or crocheting delicate laces, and she began to feel that people needed not only enough food to eat, and safe conditions in which they could work, but also a chance to create beautiful things with their hands and a chance to see beautiful pictures and to hear good music. All of these things Jane Addams remembered when, years later, her dream house came true.

One day in Europe she stood in an old cathedral and looked at the wonderful stained-glass windows. In those windows were pictures of some of the early saints of the church, alongside pictures of Hebrew prophets and Greek thinkers—pictures of Christians, Jews and Greeks all in the same church. Then Jane Addams' dream grew bigger, for she seemed to see a "cathedral of humanity," large enough to take in all the people of the world living in peace together.

But all this time she did not know just what she could do to make her dream come true. When she came back to America, she began to make up her mind. Chicago, in those days, was a rapidly growing city. Down on Halsted Street, far away from the lake, there had settled many immigrants from European countries. Once there had been beautiful homes on this street, where rich people lived, but they had long since left these homes and had moved out into the country. These houses were now old and run down; they had been made over into shops and small tenements for the poor. Italians, Bohemians, German Jews, Poles, Russians and Irish were now living in these tenements. Whole families were crowded into one or two rooms.

There on Halsted Street, right in the midst of all these strangers from across the sea, Miss Addams bought a house that had once belonged to a man by the name of Hull. So, the people called it Hull House. She invited a few of her friends to come and live with her and they began to make friends with all the people who lived in that section around them. Miss Addams remembered the fun she and her brother had playing when they were children. They had had the whole countryside to play in, but the children on Halsted Street had only narrow dirty streets in which to play. So Miss Addams invited the boys and girls to come into Hull House, and she and her friends helped them to organize clubs, and they set aside rooms in Hull House where the children could play games and where they could make things with their hands. Miss Addams also persuaded a rich man to give a tract of land for a playground. It is said to have been the first public playground in this country.

She remembered, too, how the people of Europe loved beautiful things. So, she persuaded another friend to build a special building to hold good paintings, and art exhibits were held there for the people to see when they were through with their work. Miss Addams knew that back in Bohemia and Germany these people had loved to dance the folk dances of their country. So Hull House had dances at which in the evenings the people taught each other their folk dances. Miss Addams knew that many of the older women, back in the countries from which they came, had had big looms in their houses, on which they had woven beautiful cloth. Now they were crowded in one or two small rooms in the tenements and could not have their looms. So, she bought looms and had them set up in Hull House where the women could come and weave their lovely patterns as they had done in their old homes. In these ways Miss Addams helped to keep her neighbors from being homesick and made them glad to be American citizens.

All the time Miss Addams and her friends who lived with her at Hull House were trying to get laws passed to make working conditions better for people and to see that the milk supply of Chicago was made pure and clean and to secure more playgrounds for boys and girls. The people around Hull House came to think of it as their second home. Whenever they needed help of any kind they came to Hull House, and always they found someone there ready to listen to them or to go to their homes in case of illness or accident or trouble of any kind.

So much did Jane Addams want her dreams to come true that she was willing to be misunderstood and to be talked about bitterly. It mattered not so long as she believed her cause was right. When the first world war came, Miss Addams remembered her dream in the German cathedral so many years before, a dream that all men should live in peace, and worship God together—each in his own way. She refused to believe that it was right for America to go into the war. This turned many of her friends against her and there were times when she probably felt very lonely, indeed. But that did not make her change her belief in what was right.

Up to the end of her life, she seemed to understand the dreams of other people, those of the many races who lived near Hull House and who came to it for help and understanding. Someone has written the following lines about her. They tell of Greek workmen who had once lived in Athens, near the Acropolis, but who had come to this country and who lived near Hull House and loved Jane Addams.

Some workmen, who in boyhood knew
   The glory of the sunset's beams
Upon the great Acropolis,
   Watched by her coffin. "It is true,
The only one who knew our dreams,"
   They mourned, "is dead." Did she
      hear this?
Among us whom she understood,
   Statesmen or children on the street,
Who doubts that she is yearning yet?

Ah, many love their fellow men,
   Thank God, as she did. It was hers
Uniquely hers, by radiant gleams
   Of pure imagination, then
And now, where'er her spirit stirs,
   To understand their highest dreams![7]

Prayer. A Prayer for Our City (Village or Community)

Worshipful Discussion of New Hymn (if time permits)

LEADER: Some boys and girls in a church school in New York City once were thinking, as we are, of how beautiful this earth is in many ways, but they could not forget that many places were not all good and beautiful. So, with their leader's help, they wrote the words of this hymn. Let us read the words together before we sing them.

(*After verse one*): What lines in this verse remind you of Jane Addams?

[7] From *Jane Addams, a Biography,* by James Webber Linn, D. Appleton-Century Company, 1935.

(*After verse two*) : What people did you think of as we read this verse? Or, suppose you were an artist and you wanted to paint a great picture that would help people everywhere to see clearly some of the people to whom "the world has seemed unfair." What would you paint on your canvas?

(*Before verse three*) : This last verse is about us. Find the lines that tell just how Jane Addams made her dream come true.

"Make keen our minds to plan the best."

The World One Neighborhood

We thank thee, Lord, for eyes to see
The beauty of the earth,
For ears to hear the words of love
And happy sounds of mirth
For minds that find new thoughts to think,
New wonders to explore,
For health and freedom to enjoy
The good thou hast in store.

Help us remember that to some
The eye and ear and mind
Bring sights and sounds of ugliness
And only sadness find;
Help us remember that to them
The world has seemed unfair,
That we must strive to bring to them
The beauty all may share.

O may our eyes be open, Lord,
To see our neighbor's need,
And may our ears be kept alert
Their cries for help to heed;
Make keen our minds to plan the best

> For one another's good,
> That all the world may be at last
> One friendly neighborhood.   Amen.[8]

Postlude

THIRD SERVICE OF WORSHIP

Prelude

Hymn. "Joyful, Joyful, We Adore Thee" (Sung to the tune, "Hymn of Joy" by Beethoven). Or, "Praise to the Brave, the True"

Story. "Dick Whittington Builds a Better City"

The story today is about a boy who dreamed a dream which one day came true. It is an old, old story and, as often happens, a great many legends grew up about this boy who became famous, so that it is hard to tell sometimes which parts of the story are true. But the part about his dream is a fact.

Many years ago, on a hillside in England, a boy sat looking across the fields and beyond toward the city of London. As he sat there dreaming, he almost thought he could see the spires and towers of London and hear the bells ringing throughout the city. In his dreams it seemed to him that he could hear the great bell of Bow, the bell that rang morning and evening to mark the working ours of the men of London, and the bell seemed to be saying,

"Younger son, younger son, up with stick and bundle." And in his heart the boy answered,

[8] By Jeanette E. Perkins, in *Children's Worship in the Church School,* page 182. Also in *Beacon Song and Service Book,* No. 139.

Yet will I remember, yet will I remember,
By the chivalry of God, until my day is done,
When I meet a gentle heart, lonely and unshielded,
Every barefoot boy on earth is but a younger son.[9]

Down in the valley Dick Whittington (for that was the boy's name) saw merchant travelers riding horses, with bundles of gay silks and wool packed upon their backs, and with silver bridle bells jingling as they moved along toward London town. With his stick and bundle on his shoulder, Dick Whittington ran to meet the travelers, and when they asked of him the way to Dorset, Dick led the way for them.

Down by little Kimmeridge, and up by Hampshire
        forest-roads,
Round by Sussex violets, and apple-bloom of Kent,
Singing songs of London, telling tales of London,
All the way to London, with packs of wool they
        went.[10]

At sunset Dick's heart swelled as he saw the moat of London glittering round her mighty wall. Passing through the great gate, the travelers wound their way along a winding street. They found it filled with merrymakers taking part in the Feast of St. John. Down the street came the procession. The merchant travelers reined in their horses to let the parade pass by, and, as Dick Whittington looked down from the horse on which he was riding, he saw a girl in a green

[9] From "Flos Mercatorum" by Alfred Noyes, in *Collected Poems*, Frederick A. Stokes Company, 1913, Volume II.
[10] *Ibid.*

gown, caught in the crowd and looking up with frightened eyes.

Swiftly Dick leaned down and caught the girl up on his horse, and seated her in front of him, while the trumpets pealed and the drums rolled. When the pageant had passed by, the girl in the green gown said, "Put me down at Red Rose Lane." Dick Whittington did as she asked, and the girl vanished in the crowd.

That night Dick Whittington earned his supper by rubbing down the horses at the inn, and slept on one of the packs of wool in the courtyard of the inn.

Early the next morning he was wandering up and down the streets of London, trying to find some shop where an apprentice boy was wanted. That day and all the next he wandered from shop to shop along one street after another, but found no one to take him in. At nightfall of the second day, not having had anything to eat all day long, he fell down in a faint on a doorstep in Red Rose Lane.

There Dick was found by a rich merchant, named Sir Hugh Fitzwarren, who lived on this lane and who happened to be the father of the little maid in the green gown. The cook in Sir Hugh's household said she needed a scullion, meaning a boy to wash the pots and pans. So Dick Whittington washed the pots and pans by day, and at night slept in the cellar where the rats were so bad that he took the first coin he was paid to buy a cat.

One day all was excitement in Sir Hugh's great house. A merchant ship, the *Unicorn* by name, was to sail around the world, and everyone in the household was giving some money to the captain so that he could buy some special treasure and bring it home to the one who gave the money. After each one had placed his money on the table in the great dining hall, Alice, the green-gowned maid, suddenly called out, "Wait, father, we have forgotten Dick Whittington. He has not put his money down yet." So, up from the cellar came Dick pleased that Alice should have remembered him, but what should he do? Where could he get even one coin? He stammered, "Indeed, I have no money. I spent it all on a cat."

"Then stake your cat!" cried Alice. And so it happened, that when the great merchant ship sailed out of the harbor, a black cat waved her tail proudly from the stern of the ship, and Dick Whittington was left behind wondering what the captain might bring home to him.

In the days and nights that followed, while Dick Whittington tried his best to please the cross old cook, while he scrubbed and scoured the big pots and kettles during the day, and while he fought off the hungry rats at night, he made a vow, all to himself, "If ever I have the power, I shall help—

> To build that lovelier city which is paved
> For rich and poor alike, with purest gold.[11]

One night, he said to himself, "I shall never get anywhere so long as I stay on here in this kitchen. I must be up and away to seek my fortune." So, at peep of day, he stole out of the house, with a stick and bundle on his shoulder, and it was while he was resting on a

[11] Noyes, Alfred, *op. cit.*

stone at the side of the road that the old story says he heard the bells of London ringing out.

Turn again, Whittington! Turn again, Whittington!
Flower of the Merchants, thy ship hath come home!
Trailing from her crosstrees the crimson of the sunrise,
Dragging all the glory of the sunset through the foam,

> Turn again, Whittington!
> Turn again, Whittington!
> Lord Mayor of London![12]

So, Whittington turned back and was in his place in the kitchen before the cross old cook even knew he had gone—back to scrubbing his kettles again, and wondering what the bells had been saying to him.

Finally Dick Whittington had his chance to keep his vow. One day, after many months, the ship *Unicorn* sailed home into the harbor. When the captain was about to pour his gold upon the table in the home of Sir Hugh Fitzwarren, he called for Dick Whittington. Up from the cellar again came Dick and looked with startled eyes as the captain poured out for him rubies, emeralds, diamonds and gold.

"That is the price of your cat," said the captain. "A king in Barbary, whose kingdom was infested by rats, paid this for your cat. Take it, lad, you are a rich man. See that you use your wealth wisely."

So it was that Dick Whittington kept his vow. Strange to say, some years later, he became Lord Mayor of London, as the bells had prophesied, and then he had the power to start making the dream he had often dreamed come true. He began building

[12] Noyes, Alfred, *op. cit.*

that lovelier city which is paved
For rich and poor alike, with purest gold.

London in those days, however, was far from
beautiful. Prisoners in Old Newgate Prison often died
of fever, because of the dirty, damp and dark cells
where they were held. Whittington rebuilt the prison.
Water was scarce in London. People became sick because of the foul water they had to drink. Dick Whittington had fountains made where clear fresh water
flowed for all. Sick people suffered without nurses and
doctors to care for them. Dick Whittington built the
hospital of St. Bartholomew. He built schools also,
and colleges, libraries, and homes for the old and
the weary.

Dick Whittington was helped in all these good
works by the woman he had married—Alice of the
green gown. The old story says that "night and morning, like two children still, Whittington and his Alice
bowed their heads together, praying for London, the
city of their dreams."

LEADER: If, like Dick Whittington and Alice of long
ago, we were to make a prayer for our very own city
(town, village or community) now, what things should
we want to pray for? Perhaps, the story we have just
heard has made us think of things to put in our
prayer.

The leader may embody these suggestions in a spoken
prayer. He may suggest also that we make this a grow-

ing prayer, adding to it from time to time, as we think more about our community and what it needs.

LEADER: We have a song which was written about our city and other cities like it. Let us sing the first two verses and remember that the second verse is a prayer. Like Dick Whittington and Alice, let us pray for our city.

Hymn. "The Fathers Built This City," stanzas one and two

ADDITIONAL WORSHIP MATERIALS

Story. "Character Bad"

At the outbreak of the First World War an American boy happened to be in England. On all sides of him young Englishmen were on fire with patriotism. Everybody was shouting, "Let us fight to save the world for democracy!" America was not yet in the war, but in many of the letters which came to him from home, his friends were saying that America ought to get in the war. They, too, began to talk about "saving the world for democracy."

This young man, by the name of Harold Gray, began to ask himself this question, "But, will a world war really save the world, or will it really lead to more killing and more enmity between countries?" He began to write some of his thoughts in his letters to his family back in America. He tried to make them understand that he had made up his mind that the best way to be patriotic was to refuse to fight for his country or to kill the young men of other countries. Back in America some of his friends found it very hard to understand why he thought as he did. For Harold Gray had made up his mind that it was wrong for any Christian to kill another person.

He sailed back to America and when our country entered the war Harold Gray refused to join the army. So the government put him in prison, first at Fort Leavenworth and finally at Alcatraz. Perhaps it was while he sat looking out through prison bars that Harold Gray began to dream a dream of what he could do to save America. "Save the world for democracy!" screamed the headlines in the newspapers. "Save the world for democracy!" came the echo in his own heart. But how? What could he do? He thought and thought, and gradually a plan began to shape itself in his mind.

Then, after several years, there came the day when Harold Gray was let out of prison. The war was over. The armies had gone back to their homes—all that was left of them. Many homes were sad because fathers and brothers in all the countries of the world had been killed. When Harold Gray left prison he was handed a card of dismissal and in unmistakable large letters, printed on his card, were the words, "CHARACTER BAD." So he carried out of prison with him a card that said "Character Bad," but he carried, too, the dream that he had been dreaming, of how to make his country a good place for people to live in.

He happened to be the son of a wealthy family and he decided to use his share of the money to start a community where families of young people could have comfortable homes and share in the work of the community and share in whatever businesses they would run. So he bought some land in Michigan and gathered some young fathers and mothers together and asked them if they would like to live there with him and have gardens and orchards and livestock and a dairy and a poultry farm and a canning factory where they would can the fruits and vegetables that they raised. And instead of owning all these things himself because he was the one who had the money, Mr. Gray is making it possible for all the men and women who work on the farms to own equal shares in it. It is called the Saline Valley Farms, and Mr. Gray believes that real democracy means that everybody will think, not of himself alone, but of the good of everybody else. So this is how Harold Gray is trying to make his dream come true. Instead of fighting to save the world for democracy, he is giving his life to it.

Hymns.[13] "Once to Every Man and Nation," stanzas one and two

> "God Be in My Head"
> "These Things Shall Be, a Loftier Race"
> "O Beautiful for Spacious Skies"
> "The World, Dear Lord, Is Very Large"
> "God of Our Fathers, Whose Almighty Hand"

[13] All of these hymns may be found in the *Beacon Song and Service Book*. Most of them may be found in any hymnal.

Prayers. An Early Greek Prayer

May I be no man's enemy, and may I be the friend of that which is eternal and abides. May I never quarrel with those nearest me; and if I do, may I be reconciled quickly. May I never devise evil against any man; if any devise evil against me, may I escape uninjured and without the need of hurting him. May I love, seek, and attain only that which is good. May I wish for all men's happiness and envy none. May I never rejoice in the ill fortune of one who has wronged me. When I have done or said what is wrong may I never wait for the rebuke of others, but always rebuke myself until I make amends. May I win no victory that harms either me or my opponent. May I never fail a friend in danger. May I respect myself. May I always keep tame that which rages within me. May I accustom myself to be gentle and never be angry because of circumstances.

A Prayer for Peace (By Andree P. Cadet, a thirteen-year-old student of Staten Island, New York)

For nearly three years I have been traveling around the world. Therefore, I take a strong interest in current European events.

This morning my mind wandering in the past recollects those other sunny Sunday mornings in Praha, when I awoke to the joyful chimes of church bells—or the lovely afternoons spent in some remote part of the Black Forest, drinking raw milk and thrilling at the sight of country folk in their Sunday national garb, gaily dancing.

And I shiver when I think of my little friend Hilda in Baden-Baden, and my little friend Hannah in Praha.

Today the drums of war are rolling—I leave it to other people older and more qualified than I am to discuss international problems—I am just frightened to think of what tomorrow may bring to my friends Hilda and Hannah.

My birthplace in northern France has a special cemetery

for those killed in action during the last war—French, English, Canadians, Americans, Germans. Once they fought against each other—now they lie at peace in the same land.

I am so glad to be living now in the country of freedom and peace.

I pray that war may yet be averted, so that in the plains of Hungary, in the woods of Germany, and in the mountains of Czechoslovakia the cows may graze and the birds may sing. I pray that black crosses and graves shall not desolate land-scapes where trees should grow high and flowers blossom.

2

CREATORS WITH GOD

"In the handiwork of their craft is their prayer."

In a world in which the arts of communication and of visual education are so perfected that young people are increasingly aware of the ugliness and wrong that persists in a so-called Christian civilization there is need for repeated reminder that God has always and is still expressing Himself in beauty.

Boys and girls may begin to sense that great fellowship of creative artists who have expressed this beauty in a variety of media and to realize that a conscious fellowship with God, strengthened in moments of worship, may be carried over into creative activity which enriches the lives of many people and helps them to become aware of God's presence. The experience of worship may be said to "carry over" into living when people feel that "in the handiwork of their craft is their prayer."

Since a good deal of new worship material is suggested for use in these services, it will be well to relate any new materials, such as hymns, readings, music or prayers, as vividly as possible to the story or biographical material which has been used in previous services.

If the leader will read through thoughtfully the

following selection, parts of which will be used in each service in this series, he will discover the keynote of these services.

What is so great a good as the joy of creating—
Of shaping by our own thoughts and hands the beauty which others may share?
For words that seem dull upon the lips of the crowd come alive in the mind of the poet;
They spring from his heart as a song and inspire the world.
The sounds of the earth beat upon our ears unheeded.
But one man touches the strings of a violin and our souls rise on wings of music.
Colors brilliant and dull pass before us and we care not.
But a painter brushes them upon a canvas and reveals to us hidden glories.
Ore that is dug from the earth lies formless on a shovel;
Yet it flashes in an engine as steel or is wrought into the strength and beauty of a bridge.
At the hands of man unfeeling stone rises in majesty,
And in the temple he has built man finds God.
How wonderful is the creative work of man;
How beautiful are the products of his mind and hand!
Blessed are the toilers who serve mankind by their labor,
But blessed above all are they whose hands bring forth beauty from the common things that we pass by.[1]

—Robert T. Weston

Services Of Worship

FIRST SERVICE OF WORSHIP

The introduction to this series might well be made

[1] *Beacon Song and Service Book,* Beacon Press, 1935, page 28.

through telling to the group the story of Stradivarius and associating with it George Eliot's poem, "Stradivarius."

The Story. "The Whittler of Cremona"[2]

It was May in Cremona, and carnival time. Revelers danced about the streets in holiday attire—music and gaiety were everywhere. Down a narrow alley, off the square, three boys stood in the shadow. They wore no masks, no scarlet clothing. They were poorly dressed, barefooted.

Gulio was talking. "But I tell you, Salvatore, now is the time. In the square where the crowds are we shall make money. . . . You sing, and I will play. Come."

"You are right, Gulio. I will go with you. Merry hearts make open hands, and we will make money tonight. Will you come, Tonio?"

"Yes, I'll come," Tonio answered, "even if I cannot sing. . ."

The brothers laughed. "You can do nothing but whittle," they said, "and that never earns you a penny. But come, we must hurry. People are in their merriest mood now."

Gulio picked up his violin and led the way. The holiday mood was in their hearts, too, and they frolicked and laughed as they went. But Antonio said little, for he was thinking of what the boys had said— that he could do nothing but whittle. It really made him sad because he loved music and he could do nothing

---

[2] Adapted from the story by Katherine Dunlap Cather, by Letitia Evelyn Pike. Used by Permission.

to make it. He had no violin, and when he tried to sing his voice squeaked so that the boys laughed.

Now it was carnival time and the whole world was merry, so Tonio could not be sad for long, and soon he was laughing and dancing with the others. Then they were in the square, and Gulio began to play. Salvatore's voice was sweet like a flute, and people stopped to listen. They tossed coins at the boys and Salvatore caught them in his hat.

Meantime Tonio sat on the steps of the Cathedral and whittled as he always did. When it had grown quite dark, Tonio looked up to see a tall man passing. He seemed to care little for the noise and the fun, but he stopped to listen to the boys as they played. "That was a pretty song," he said when they had finished. "Will you sing it again for a lonely old man?" The boys sang, and he handed Salvatore a gold coin, and went on without seeing Antonio at all.

"Look!" Salvatore cried. "It is gold! A gold coin from the great Amati!"

Tonio looked at the money. "Who is the great Amati?" he wanted to know.

"Amati is the great violin maker," Gulio told him. "He is the greatest in Italy, and very, very rich, they say. But he really cares for nothing but his work."

The boys were so happy over their good fortune that they decided to go home. Tonio went with them as far as the bridge. There he turned, hurried on to his own home, and crept quietly to bed. But he did not sleep for his brain was on fire with a plan. He could not sing, he could not play, he could only whittle. But right here in Cremona was a great man who whittled, too. With knives and bits of wood, he made whole violins. . . .

Before dawn, Tonio was up again. He ate a piece of bread, and then gathered up a few of the things he had made with his knife—a sheep, a fox, a camel. He crept out of the house, and soon found the way to the Great Amati's—it was not hard, for everyone, it seemed, knew where he lived. Before the matin bell had rung, Tonio stood at his door. The servant opened it, but he scolded crossly when he saw that it was only a boy who stood there. The master could not be disturbed so early. So Tonio went away, and waited a little. Then he came back and rattled the big knocker again. Again the servant was about to send him away, but the master heard the angry voices and came to see what was the matter.

"I have brought these things for you to see," Tonio pleaded. "I cut them with my knife, and I want to know if you think I could make violins."

The great man smiled. "What is your name, my lad?" he asked.

"Antonius Stradivarius."

"And why do you want to make violins?"

"Because I love music," Tonio told him. "But I cannot make any. I can neither sing nor play as Gulio and Salvatore do. I can do nothing but whittle."

The master laid his hand on Tonio's shoulder. "Come in and try," he said. "For the song in the heart is all that matters. There are many ways of making music. Some play violins, some paint pictures and make statues. Others till the soil to make the flowers bloom. And each is singing his own song, and helping to make music for the world. . . . The song you sing with your knives and wood will be just as noble as the ones Salvatore and Gulio sing with voice and violin."

So Tonio Stradivarius, the boy who could not sing, became the pupil of the great Amati. He worked hard, day after day, month after month, often when he would rather run and play. Years passed, and Tonio still cut and shaped, and placed the strings, with the song still in his heart, and the skill growing in his fingers.

That was more than two hundred years ago, and to this day, the greatest of musicians, those who can afford them, use Stradivarius violins. They are very rare and costly, and their tones are mellow and sweet. People often ask how the music they make can be so rich and so clear. If Tonio were here he would tell them that it was very simple. It is because they were made with the song in his heart, and the skill in the fingers of a boy who could never sing or play, but could only whittle.

———————— is going to play for us on a violin as we think of the boy Stradivarius and how he made music for the world because there was a song in his heart.

Violin Solo

Reading of the poem

If possible copies of the poem ³ should be in the

³ The poem may be found in the *Beacon Song and Service Book,* page 69.

hands of every pupil while the leader first reads it aloud to the group.

Stradivarius

Your soul was lifted by the wings today
Hearing the master of the violin.
But did you think
Of old Antonio Stradivari?—him
Who a good century and a half ago
Put his true work in that brown instrument
And by the nice adjustment of its frame
Gave it responsive life, continuous
With the master's finger-tips and perfected
Like them by delicate rectitude of use.
No simpler man than he: he never cried,
"Why was I born to this monotonous task
Of making violins?"
"When my master holds
'Twixt chin and hand a violin of mine,
He will be glad that Stradivari lived,
Made violins, and made them of the best.
The masters only know whose work is good:
They will choose mine, and, while God gives them skill,
I give them instruments to play upon,
God choosing men to help him.
"If my hand slacked
I should rob God—since he is fullest good—
Leaving a blank instead of violins.
" 'Tis God gives skill,
But not without men's hand: he could not make
Antonio Stradivari's violins
Without Antonio."[4]

Conversation. Are there other beautiful things which we enjoy that depend upon the skill and careful work of artisans?

[4] By George Eliot (Mary Ann Evans Cross).

If there is any beautiful ironwork in the church, the story of Frank Koralewsky from "The Goldsmith of Florence," by Katherine Gibson will show how painstakingly he had to work as an apprentice to learn his craft.

Children's replies may mention not only artisans but artists, poets, painters and composers. The leader may suggest that on future Sundays they will hear about some of these other creators of beauty.

SECOND SERVICE OF WORSHIP

Prelude

Hymn. "God of the Earth, the Sky, the Sea"

Call to Worship

LEADER: O worship God who is the creator of beauty. Open your eyes and the whole world is full of God.

RESPONSE (Unison): Praise God for beauty everywhere,

Praise God for love that all may share.[5]

A Fragment of an Old Play (Dramatized by two boys)

THE DUKE: (*to a man at work in the Plazza Vecchio*) How come you here?
THE MAN: I await my companions, sire.
THE DUKE: Ah, the frescoes; yes. And the box you are making for pastime, how will it be used?
THE MAN: Flowers will be planted in it, sire.
THE DUKE: It will be filled with dirt. Why take such pains with it, to make each joint and surface perfect?
THE MAN: I love perfect things.

[5] Used by permission of Beacon Press.

THE DUKE: Eh? It is wasted effort. No one will observe its perfection. Its usage does not require such perfection.

THE MAN: But my spirit does.

THE DUKE (*scowling*) Sirrah, what?

THE MAN: Do you suppose that the Carpenter of Nazareth ever made anything less well than he could? That he was ever satisfied with anything less perfect than it could be made?

THE DUKE: (*angrily*) Sacrilege! Fellow, you shall be flogged. What is your name?

THE MAN: Michelangelo, sire.

Unison Reading. "The Joy of Creating"

What is so great a good as the joy of creating—
Of shaping by our own thoughts and hands the beauty
      which others may share?
For words that seem dull upon the lips of the crowd
      come alive in the mind of the poet;
They spring from his heart as a song and inspire
      the world.
The sounds of the earth beat upon our ears unheeded,
But one man touches the strings of a violin and our souls
      rise on wings of music.

Hymn. "Now Praise We Great and Famous Men."

Now praise we great and famous men,
The fathers named in story;
And praise the Lord who now as then
Reveals in man his glory.

Praise we the great of heart and mind,
The singers sweetly gifted,
Whose music like a mighty wind
The souls of men uplifted.

Praise we the peaceful men of skill
Who builded homes of beauty,

And, rich in art, made richer still
The brotherhood of duty.

In peace their sacred ashes rest,
Fulfilled their day's endeavor;
They blessed the earth, and they are blessed
Of God and man forever.[6]

THIRD SERVICE OF WORSHIP

Begin this service with the enjoyment of a few pictures such as "The Angelus" by Millet and "Hilltop at Nazareth" by Elsie Anna Wood. After looking at the pictures, talk about the different aspects of prayer which each of these painters has tried to portray. Reread the unison reading, "The Joy of Creating," used in the previous service and then read together, pausing after the reading for a moment of appreciation, the next couplet.

Colors brilliant and dull pass before us and we care
   not,
But a painter brushes them upon a canvas and reveals
   to us hidden glories.

If possible have a large copy of the picture, "Praying Hands" by Albrecht Dürer, hanging before the group as a center for the service of worship.

Picture Interpretation. "Praying Hands" by Albrecht Dürer.

School was out in the quaint old city of Nürnberg in Germany. A twelve-year-old boy, with his books under

[6] By William G. Tarrant, in *Beacon Song and Service Book*, Beacon Press, 1935, No. 143.

his arm, was walking home from school ever so slowly. A good many things were happening to him on this particular day. In the first place he was twelve years old, and in those days it meant that a boy was through with his schooling. But the day meant something else too. For Albrecht Dürer on the very next day would start in at his father's workshop as his father's apprentice to learn the trade of a goldsmith. Albrecht would enjoy this, but not so much as his father, who had been looking forward for a long time to the day when his son would begin to work with him and learn his craft. The boy was bright and very clever with his hands, and his father felt sure that he would make an expert worker in metals.

But Albrecht had already set his heart on being a painter. And that was one reason he was walking so slowly from school. For his way led right past the studio of the great painter, Wohlgemuth, and he loved to look in the windows and imagine himself as an apprentice in the great master's studio.

But in spite of his secret longing, the next morning he started in learning his father's trade and so quick was he and so skillful with his hands that before long he was doing work that made his father very proud. Yet, all the time, Albrecht kept wishing that he could learn to paint and whenever he had a spare minute he would get out his crayons and paper and draw pictures.

Finally, one day, he got up courage enough to ask his father if he might learn to be a painter instead of a goldsmith. At first his father was very much disappointed, but all he said to Albrecht was, "Bring out some of your drawings and let me see how good you are." The moment he saw them he knew that the boy would make a great painter if only he studied with a good teacher. One of the drawings was one which the boy had done of himself. Some day if you go to Europe and visit Dürer's own house in the old city of Nürnberg, you will be able to see for yourself this drawing of Dürer's. On the back of it he has written, "I portrayed this after my own image in a glass in the year 1484 when I was still a child."

So his father let Albrecht go to the studio of the great Wohlgemuth and become an apprentice, and a very happy boy joined the other apprentices and began to learn the art of painting. It was hard work and it was true, as his father had said, that it did not bring in much money for a long time. But Dürer did not care as long as he was doing the thing that he most wanted to do.

The day finally came, after years of work, when Dürer became known as one of the great painters of Germany. But while he was working hard to become a great artist, he earned money by making all sorts of drawings and paintings and woodcuts for people. In those days there were few books and people had to get their stories from pictures. Dürer drew lovely flowers and little animals and horsemen and landscapes, and most of all, Bible stories which he engraved on copper and then made copies of to be sold at the church doors.

One of the pictures which people all over the world have admired is "The Praying Hands." As we look at it we wonder whose hands they were. Were they those of a priest in one of the churches? Were they the work-worn hands of some peasant, dropping into the back of a cathedral at the close of a long day of work to offer his evening prayer? There is a story told which says that Dürer had a friend who also wanted to be an artist and that both he and Dürer were very, very poor, so poor that they did not have enough to eat. So, the friend said, "I will go and get a job and earn money for us to live on while you learn to become a painter and when you have learned and can earn money for us, then I will take lessons." But the years went by and when Dürer was ready to support his friend, the friend's hands were too stiff from his hard labor to hold a paintbrush. So Dürer said, "Out of gratitude to my friend, I will paint his hands in the attitude of prayer." Of Dürer's friend, as of Dürer, it could be said that "in the handiwork of their craft was their prayer."

Unison Reading. "What is so great a good as the joy of creating?"

Hymn. "Now Praise We Great and Famous Men"

FOURTH SERVICE OF WORSHIP

This service of worship, too, centers in the appreciation of pictures. The entire set of Beneker's pictures of workmen can be secured from Mrs. Flora Beneker, Truro, Massachusetts. The only one which can be purchased separately is "Men Are Square." If this is the only one available, let it hang where all can seĕ it. The picture most usable for this service is "The Builder." There is a small reproduction of this in Bailey's *Art and Character*, plate 168. In the pre-session period, the book might lie on the browsing table and the boys and girls be directed to look at the picture as they enter. Then, the leader can so describe it that they will readily visualize it during the service. Or the picture in the book may be thrown on a screen by a projector.

MATERIALS APPROPRIATE FOR THIS SERVICE

Unison Reading. "What is so great a good as the joy of creating?"

Add the next two lines:

Ore that is dug from the earth lies formless on a shovel;
Yet it flashes in an engine as steel or is wrought into
      the strength and beauty of a bridge.

Hymns. 1. "In Praise of Workers" (To the tune of "For the Beauty of the Earth")

> For the workers in the mill
>   For the craftsmen and their art;
> For the builder's ready skill
>   And the tradesman in the mart;
> Lord of all, for them we raise
> This our hymn of grateful praise.
>
> For the toilers on the farm,
>   For the sailors on the sea;
> For the miners' strength of arm
>   We shall ever thankful be.

Lord of all, for them we raise
This our hymn of grateful praise.[7]

2. "Hail the Hero Workers."

Prayers. A prayer with moments of silence after each sentence.

Our Father God, Creator of beautiful things
We are thankful for the lovely things we see: faces, pictures, flowers, trees, prairies, waves, and running water.

. . . .

We are thankful for the lovely things we hear; kind words and laughter; stories and beautiful poems; songs and music of pianos, violins, and orchestras.

. . . .

We are thankful that we can sing and draw and paint and use tools, and so make beautiful things ourselves.

. . . .

We are thankful that we can bring happiness to others by giving them beautiful and useful things that we have made.

. . . .

We want to do good work when we make something, and to finish what we begin. Amen.[8]

Story Material to Interpret Beneker's pictures

A few years ago there lived in the little New England village of Truro on Cape Cod a young painter by the name of Gerrit Beneker. The people whom he liked best to paint in all the world were strong working-

[7] By Miriam Petersen, in *Children's Worship in the Church School*, by Jeanette E. Perkins, Harper & Brothers, 1939, page 180.
[8] From *Beacon Song and Service Book,* page 90.

men like the one in the picture before us. When he was a little boy he must have stood for hours watching the men on the tops of tall skyscrapers, riveting the iron girders or hoisting the heavy beams into place. Somehow, it seemed to him that this was wonderful work, erecting great buildings where thousands of men would work every day; making everything in those buildings true and safe, so that no harm would come to anyone. And it was dangerous work, too. What if that man hanging up there so high should slip just a little bit and fall to his death? Was he ever afraid? And what hard work it was! Could that man way up there among the steel girders sing the Song of Labor?

> List to the Lark!
> He soars and sings,
> Wake to your work,
> The Matin rings!
> Praise God for work![9]

As Beneker grew older he made friends with many workmen and the better he knew them the more he admired them. He was proud that some of these strong workmen were his friends. He decided to paint the pictures of some of his workmen friends so that he could show other people by his pictures how true and faithful they were in their work. In many companies in our country workmen do not have proper working conditions. Some of them do not receive enough money for the hard and dangerous work that they do. Beneker thought something like this, "If I paint some pictures showing that workmen are square, perhaps the men

[9] Clarence Dickinson, *The Norfolk Chimes*, H. W. Gray Company.

who employ them will see the pictures and will work with the laboring men to get better working conditions for them." Beneker thought, too, that we would have a more beautiful America if the men who have money and who own the factories and the men who work in them would both work together to build a better world where all men could be happy.

So, he went into a steel mill in Cleveland and painted a number of pictures of his friends, the workingmen. One was of an engineer, one of some men welding and one, this picture, which he called "Men Are Square." When the leaders of the American Federation of Labor saw this picture, they said, "That is what we think the best workingmen look like. We would like the American people to realize how square workingmen are." So they hung this picture in a great exposition hall in Philadelphia where all people who went through could look at it.

In his picture "The Builder," Beneker has given us a picture of a workingman who is a dreamer. It is near sunset and time for the men to quit work. A strong young workmen is standing on a steel beam five hundred feet in the air. He has stopped a minute to think about his work and suddenly it seems to him that he sees a vision in the sunset. He straightens up, takes off his hat and looks up at the sky. All day he has been too busy at his hard work to think, but he suddenly realizes how wonderful is the work of a builder. Below him in the great city are all the works of the past, built by other builders. Here, he is standing on a work of the present which he is helping to build. And in the sunset glory he seems to see a vision of all the beautiful cities that men can build in the future—cities in which all men and women and little children shall have enough to eat and leisure time in which to be happy. That will be a city "undimmed by human tears," as our song, "America the Beautiful," says. And this young builder may be saying a prayer of Thanksgiving to God that he can have a share in building America the Beautiful.[10]

FIFTH SERVICE OF WORSHIP

Introduce this service by looking at pictures of mediaeval cathedrals and talking about the way in which they were built over a period of years. Bring out the fact that the cathedral was really a storybook to the people who worshiped in it, since most of them could not read and books were available only to the rich. So the story of religion was told in stained-glass windows, stonework and wood carving.

If possible have a large picture of Rheims Cathedral to accompany the story of "The Boy Knight of Rheims."

Explain, or let the boys and girls tell about, the mediaeval guilds and the system of apprenticeship.

MATERIALS FOR THIS SERVICE

A Psalm of Labor (From the Apocrypha)

The life of him that laboreth, and is wise
Shall be made sweet.

So is the man sitting by the anvil,
And considering the unwrought iron.

[10] Adapted from material in *Art and Character*, by Albert E. Bailey, Abingdon-Cokesbury Press, 1938.

He will set his heart upon perfecting his works,
And turning the wheel about;

He will fashion the clay with his arm,
He will apply his heart to finish the glazing.

They shall not labor in vain,
For their labor is with wisdom and with knowledge
and with skillfulness.

All these put their trust in their hands;
And each becometh wise in his own work.

For these maintain the fabric of the world;
And in the handiwork of their craft is their prayer.

Story. "The Boy Knight of Rheims"[11]

The first thing that wakened Jean d'Orbais that spring morning was the chiming of the cathedral bells just outside his window. He ran to the window, flung it wide open, climbed upon the window seat and leaned out. And there, right opposite his window was the great cathedral that he loved. Day and night Jean would lean out of that window and look and look at the statues of saints and heroes that framed the great north doorway. All around the cathedral they stood, high up in their little niches. And Jean knew every one of them as if he had carved them himself. For had not his own ancestor, the first Jean d'Orbais, planned the whole cathedral and built the apse himself? His mother had told him the story of the first Jean

[11] Adapted from the book, *The Boy Knight of Rheims*, by Eloise Lownsbery, Houghton Mifflin Company, 1927.

d'Orbais, how, since he was an orphan boy, he had been brought up by the monks and taught the trade of a builder and how his dream was some day to build a great cathedral which should reach to the sky. His dream had come true and when the first cathedral at Rheims had burned, he had been called and asked to be the Master Builder. He had thought of the people who had no books to read and couldn't read them if they had, so he wanted the cathedral to be a gigantic picture book in stone, with all the stories carved so that everyone could see. And above all else he thought of God and that if he could make his cathedral beautiful enough, men would worship God in it for hundreds of years to come.

Now, just the day before this, little Jean had been told by his father and his grandfather that he was old enough to become an apprentice, to learn a craft all his own. In a way he was very happy about it and as he leaned out of his window this spring morning, he waved his hand to the statues across the way and called out. "Good day to you all." Then he added, "I'm going to begin. I'm going to be one of the great builders."

But suddenly he remembered that he was not as happy as he wished he were. And the reason was this. Jean loved the cathedral and every statue on it. He also, like his father, loved to model in clay and he looked forward to the day when he should become a stone carver, as his father was, and some day carve statues that would fill the empty niches in the cathedral. In every generation there had been some member of the d'Orbais family carving statues for the cathedral.

And Jean, even now, had his own little pile of clay and lovingly he had modeled first one and then another of the statues of the kings and saints over the doorway of the cathedral. His family thought they were well done for a lad of his age and Jean loved to set them out before the fire and look at them as he dreamed of the big day when he could carve big ones from stone. So always he had had in his heart the hope that when he was old enough to learn a craft, he would be apprenticed to his father and work with him in his workshop right under the shadow of the cathedral that he loved.

However, the day before, his family had apprenticed him instead to Master Anton, a goldsmith, a friend of his grandfather's. They had done this because they thought that perhaps Jean would do better working in the delicate metals, making candlesticks and beautiful basins. These could be used in the cathedral, but it was not the thing that Jean most wanted to do; it was not really working on his loved cathedral. But Jean did not want to disappoint old Grandpère, who belonged to the guild of goldsmiths. So he had kept his disappointment to himself.

The days that followed were not altogether happy ones. Jean had to leave home and go to Master Anton's shop in the near-by city. He worked hard and every day did better and better work. But there was one thing that bothered him. He saw rich people come to Master Anton's shop and give him orders to make gold vessels for them and then, one day, he and Colin, the other apprentice, saw Master Anton drop something into the molten metal, something that did not look like gold. Now, the laws of the guilds were very strict and the members took solemn oaths that they would be good and honest craftsmen. So Jean knew that Master Anton was not making his vessels of good gold. Should he tell? But whom? Would they believe him, just a boy? And would it not be a terrible disappointment to Grandpère, to discover that his old friend, Master Anton, was breaking the laws of the guild?

Day after day went by and Jean said nothing about his discovery to anyone. The happiest hour of the whole week was when Saturday came and he put his few clothes in a bundle and started on the long walk home to his own family where he spent the week ends. And what happy week ends they were! He forgot all about Master Anton and his dishonesty, for he and his friend, Marcel, had a secret. Marcel had become apprenticed to Jean's father and both boys loved to model in clay and to carve stone. So they had built a sort of shack, right up against the side of the cathedral at the back and here they spent their Sundays and every fete day. They were making a life-size statue of King Clovis, an exact copy of one of the statues which the first Jean d'Orbais had made for the cathedral. The boys told no one what they were doing for they wanted to keep it a secret until it was finished and besides, it was against the law to work on Sundays and fete days.

One day Master Anton sent Jean on an errand to the home of a beautiful countess to collect some money and while Jean was there the countess took him into her chapel and showed him the stained-glass windows that had been made by Jean's own uncle. Suddenly the countess asked, "Are you happy to be a goldsmith?"

"No," said Jean. "It was Grandpère's wish, but my heart is not in it."

"What is it that your heart asks you to do?" asked the countess.

"I model," said Jean modestly. "But some day I mean to be one of the cathedral's great sculptors."

The countess smiled. "You are right to make the most of this gift," she said. "It is a great gift and the more you work at it the better. Say to yourself over and over 'I will be a great sculptor. I am part of the cathedral sculptors' and then nothing can stop you."

A few days after this, one day when Jean was working in his shack on his statue of Clovis, Marcel suddenly appeared with three rough boys and demanded that Jean give up the shack to them, as they wanted it for a clubhouse. Jean refused. Then Marcel struck the beautiful statue of Clovis so hard that the head fell to the ground. But that was not all. He struck Jean, too, and then, when he saw that Jean was unconscious, he was so frightened that he ran away.

After a long time Jean partly awoke. Though his head was racked with pain, he managed to drag himself into the cathedral and there he sat leaning against one of the great pillars in the side aisle. Strange thoughts went through his mind. He thought the carved angels from the outside had come floating into the cathedral from their niches and they seemed to be saying, "Do not blame Marcel. Forgive him, forgive him."

Then, Jean saw a figure that looked like the first Jean d'Orbais. He was smiling at Jean. Again the angels chanted, "He wants to tell you the secret of the cathedral."

The man spoke and said, "This is the secret of the cathedral.

> Men learn of God through Beauty. We Builders who
>   Hold Beauty in our fingers have the key.
>   We could create it only as we loved enough.
> We chose God as our partner: He chose us.
>   So was this cathedral builded stone on stone,
>   Each carved with the beauty of a soul and God."[12]

Suddenly Jean knew that it was like a sort of secret brotherhood, this great company of those who had tried to create beauty. The voice went on,

> "Wars may come, or raging fires, my son,
>   But yet these towers and walls will ever stand;
>   For they were builded unto Eternity,
> And even if crushed down would rise again—
>   For eager hand and hearts would catch the vision then,
>   And build them into Beauty that is God."[13]

And Jean d'Orbais *was* taken into the secret brotherhood. For when he left the cathedral and managed to make his way home, he found his family full of excitement. Master Anton had been found out and Jean was told that he need no longer be a goldsmith but could become his father's apprentice. Carefully and lovingly Jean put the head back on his statue of Clovis and when his father and the Bishop saw it, *they* knew that *Jean* knew the secret of the cathedral.

[12] From *The Boy Knight of Rheims*, by Eloise Lownsbery, Houghton Mifflin Company, 1927, page 239.
[13] *Ibid.*

His father said proudly, "You shall work with me on the carving. There will be plenty of work for us these next two years until the towers are finished, and after that the rest of our lives on the interior."

Every morning, as Jean started on his work in the studio, he would say over and over to himself: "I shall be one of her great sculptors. I walk with Beauty. I live with Beauty."

Hymns. Select hymns from those used in previous services.

Unison Reading. Add new lines to this reading.

At the hands of man unfeeling stone rises in majesty,
And in the temple he has built man finds God.

How wonderful is the creative work of man;
How beautiful are the products of his mind and hand!

Blessed are the toilers who serve mankind by their labor.
But blessed above all are they whose hands bring forth beauty from the common things that we pass by.

3

OUR FRIENDS

"This is the church of my dreams;
. . . .
A friendly church for all people,
The church of the living God."

The world of play is a very real world to boys and· girls, and the years between eight and fourteen mark a period when playmates largely fill the horizon of thought and feeling. Children of this age are not introspective as to the values of friendship. They accept the social groupings which their environment provides most easily and naturally. In most cases, the neighborhood forms the natural unit for group play life. Occasionally, other groups such as Boy or Girl Scouts offer such interesting programs and so successfully challenge the loyal participation of the boys and girls that they become what Dimock calls "primary" groups—primary, in that they elicit from young people their wholehearted interest and devotion. Within such "primary" groups, whether of the neighborhood or of some other organization, each boy or girl has certain companions with whom he has formed closer friendships than with others.

To measure up to the full stature of friendship is a matter of slow growth and one which demands understanding adult guidance. In a world in which competition has become a recognized motive for success, there is need for an appreciation of friendly relations in which we recognize that, "it is not well for any one of us until it is well for all of us."

When the child leaves the home and neighborhood group to enter the school community, he is immediately placed in a position in which he must of necessity compete with the abilities of others, in matters of physical, intellectual and social achievement.

With these aspects of the child's social life in mind, the church group may help him in the following ways.

1. The church has an opportunity to substitute, in the group life which it offers the child, co-operation for competition. The boy or girl should have a feeling of security in his church group. It should be for him a friendly, happy group in which he looks upon all the other members of it, not as competitors, but as loyal friends devoted to the common good. Teachers and leaders of worship are responsible for creating such a group life so that all may be able to sing sincerely,

> It is my joy in life to find
> At every turning of the road,
> The strong arm of a comrade kind,
> To help me onward with my load.[1]

2. Church leaders should try to help the child, in a practical way, to learn to live co-operatively in a social group. Dr. Ernest Chave speaks of the necessity "to find the right balance between self-respect and

[1] By Frank D. Sherman, in *The American Student Hymnal*, H. Augustine Smith, Editor. D. Appleton-Century Company, 1928.

self-confidence and respect for the rights and values of others."[2]

3. Boys and girls should be encouraged to show genuine kindliness to many kinds of people.

> a. To new boys and girls in the neighborhood, school or church.
>
> b. To any with handicaps of size or physical disability.
>
> c. To those of other races.

4. Gradually there should develop an expansion of the area of their friendships to include younger boys and girls, older people and other social groups than their own.

In any one area, like this of friendship, the church school cannot expect or be expected to help the child solve all the problems involved. Home and school should carry their share of accomplishing the total objectives. But, in each area of experience, there are certain objectives for which the church is especially fitted to work.

Neither is it to be expected that the experience of worship, apart from other aspects of the program of religious education, can solve the difficulties. It is inconsistent to ask a group of boys and girls to express gratitude for friends who help us and stand by us if, within their church-school group, there are petty jealousies and unfriendly acts. Neither can they very well envisage a friendly world-community, unless the church itself is a fellowship of friendly persons.

The following services, if they are undergirded by

[2] In *Personality Development of Children*, by Ernest Chave, University of Chicago Press, 1937.

the actual experiencing of a happy, friendly church group-life, may serve to deepen the group's worship of God. They can do this by emphasizing the values inherent in true friendship and the possibility of making the church a happy fellowship of Christians.

Junior boys and girls want to be liked and to be included in their social groups. They feel it keenly when they are left out, but they easily forget when they are on the inside. So they are often unwittingly cruel to other boys and girls, because they fail to imagine themselves in the other person's place. Juniors are easily influenced by the situations in which they find themselves, and because they are driven by powerful inborn urges to satisfy their immediate desires, they often fail to be friendly.

For this reason, a friendship project which will capture their imaginations and keep the ideal before them for a period of several weeks may help them to work consecutively at the task of being a friend. If the entire junior group is banded together in the enthusiastic endeavor to make *their* church, *their* junior department, *their* class a friendship circle in which it is a violation of the code of friendship to be unfriendly to anyone and in which they feel that it is the highest honor to be known as the "Junior Church of the Friendly Spirit," an attitude may be cultivated which will carry over into the work of the entire year.

SERVICES OF WORSHIP

FIRST SERVICE OF WORSHIP

Read the following poem together.

The little trail of being friends
Is one that never ends.
Upon it you may travel far
To where the nicest places are!
It holds for you great vistas fair
And sunlit fields and fragrant air
And better views around the bends;
The little trail of being friends.[3]

Suggest the fun and adventure of following a trail. Many of us will follow (or have followed) real trails through woods or mountains. Let us imagine we are following this trail. Where will it lead us to find friends? To our playgrounds, our neighborhoods, our homes and our vacation spots. Can we imagine who will be some of the people we shall meet along the trail? Playmates, old friends, new friends we make when we are visiting, the stranger who visits in our own neighborhood, our younger brothers and sisters, all the younger children on our street or in our neighborhood or some older people.

Discussion. "What is a friend?"

After responses from children, the leader may suggest a few definitions of a friend, as:

"A friend is one who knows all about us and likes us just the same."

A loyal friend,
One tried and true,
To give advice
Encourage you.

"To have friends, one must show himself friendly."

[3] Mary Carolyn Davies. Source unknown.

Story. "The Story of a Friend"

Once upon a time there was born in a very beautiful home a baby girl. From the moment of her birth she was surrounded by everything that money could buy. As she grew up, she was sent to the finest schools; she had two beautiful homes, one in New York City and one on the Hudson River; she was able to travel to all parts of the world and to see many interesting places and to meet interesting people of every nation. But these were not the things that people remembered about her. Her name was Grace Dodge and the one thing people thought of, when anyone said her name, was the word "Friend."

For Grace Dodge decided that the one thing in all the world which mattered most was being a friend to people who needed friends. Now, Miss Dodge said to herself, "If I want to be a friend, I will have to find what is the best way to be one." So she went to work to discover how to be a friend. She saw hundreds of working girls, girls who worked long hours in factories, girls who had very little fun, no money to spend and who, after their long working hours, were sometimes too tired to enjoy anything. And Miss Dodge said to herself, "I can never be a real friend to these girls if I have everything that money can buy and live an easy life, while they work so hard." So she decided to work as hard as any working girl. She started clubs for them where they could learn how to keep well and strong, how to dress, how to use their money wisely, how they could make friends and be happy. She started schools and night schools where girls could learn to cook and sew, for the public schools did not teach these things in those days.

She spent hours managing her money and planning where she could give it so it would do the most good. And she wrote thousands of letters to the girls she knew all over the world, girls that were lonely, girls that needed her help, girls of every race. Sometimes, after a busy day, she would sit up until late at night writing these letters, even though the writing was very painful, as she had what is called "writer's cramp." Because she knew that she ought to work as hard as all other hard-working people, she allowed herself only two weeks vacation each year. "I, too, am a working girl," she used to say, "only I happen to have had my wages paid in advance."

There was another secret of being a friend that Miss Dodge discovered. "If you have friends," she thought to herself, "you invite them to your own home." So Miss Dodge brought to her beautiful home, overlooking the Hudson River, many, many girls who never had a chance to rest and look at beautiful things. Here for week ends she brought factory girls, tired sewing women, young artists who were not earning much money and college students from China and Japan and other far-away countries who felt strange and lonely here in America. As they drove up to the door of "Greystone" (that was the name of her Hudson River home), Miss Dodge would grasp their hands and smile a welcome so that they felt they were her honored guests and she was glad to see them.

There was still one more secret of friendship which

Miss Dodge discovered. "A friend," she said, "is one who knows all about us and loves us just the same." And because all her friends knew that Miss Dodge would never turn against them no matter what they did, they came to her and told her their troubles. If they had done wrong, she helped them to start over again and do the right thing. She believed in her friends and because she believed they would be fine and honest and brave, many of them began to believe in themselves.

On the Christmas morning when Miss Dodge died, her home was filled with lonely people from lands across the sea, so that it was then, as always, a House of Friendship. "Then there were heard in factory and office, in school and home, in city and country, in the homeland and far-away lands, the voices of the strong and weak, the great and little, the rich and poor, saying, 'We have lost a friend.' And some said, 'We shall never again hear the word friend without thinking of Miss Dodge.' "[4]

LEADER: Many a working girl knew what it was to have a loyal friend when she came to know Miss Grace Dodge. The following poem probably says what many of Miss Dodge's friends felt.

Poem.

> It is my joy in life to find
> At every turning of the road,
> The strong arm of a comrade kind
> To help me onward with my load.

[4] From "The Story of a Friend," in *Comrades in Service,* by Margaret E. Burton, Missionary Education Movement, page 179.

And since I have no gold to give
And love alone must make amends,
My only prayer is, while I live,
God make me worthy of my friends![5]

Story Incident (to be linked with the last verse of the poem)

Once there lived in Russia a girl named Marie. She was such an interesting girl, so full of life, so friendly that she had many friends and people who heard about her wanted to know her. One day some people called who had never met her. A friend said to her, "There are some people here who want to meet you." Before she entered the room where the people were waiting to meet her, Marie stopped for a moment and said a little prayer, "O God, make me worth meeting."

Hymn. "I Would Be True."[6]

SECOND SERVICE OF WORSHIP

In order to stimulate thinking and discussion, it is suggested that this service begin directly with the story and lead the group gradually to the point where they feel like praying.

Story. "Mr. Friend-o'-Man's Party"[7]

When Mr. Friend-o'-Man came to the city of As-

[5] By Frank D. Sherman, *American Student Hymnal*, H. Augustine Smith, Ed., D. Appleton-Century Company, 1928, page 190.

[6] No. 105 in *Beacon Song and Service Book*; also found in many other hymnals.

[7] From *Mr. Friend-o'-Man*, by Jay T. Stocking, Missionary Education Movement.

It-Is, everybody was curious to see him and Mrs. Friend-o'-Man. The people called and left their cards, and gave the Friend-o'-Mans many invitations to dinners and parties and balls.

After awhile a lady remarked to Mrs. Friend-o'-Man that she supposed they would have a housewarming and give a grand party. Mrs. Friend-o'-Man said she thought it would be delightful.

That very night she consulted her husband. It was agreed that she should have a housewarming and give a grand party. But they did not know just how to proceed.

Ever since Mr. Friend-o'-Man had come to town, he had frequently heard the words, "the best people." When the grocer called and asked for his trade, he said, "The best people trade with me." When the marketman came he said, "The best people buy of me." When the president of the club invited them to join, he said, "The best people all belong." On the very first Sunday morning after Mr. Friend-o'-Man came to town he was told that the best people went to the big beautiful church on the hill. Mr. Friend-o'-Man had never made out how they decided who the best people were.

Mr. Friend-o'-Man thought and thought. Finally his face lighted. He had an idea that he thought might work. He sent for the newspaper reporter, who came promptly.

"When you called," said Mr. Friend-o'-Man, "you were good enough to say that you would be glad to help me at any time, did you not?"

"Certainly," said the reporter. "I am glad you remember. What can I do for you?"

"I want to find out who are the very best people in this town; not those who go to your best parties and are *labeled* your best people, but those who really are *the best*. How would a newspaper contest do?"

"Fine!" said the reporter. "How shall we manage it?"

They at once agreed on a plan that seemed very fair indeed. They called it the "Who's Who Contest."

On an appointed day, the city newspaper contained, in a corner of the first page, the following verses, with space for the signing of names, and full directions for voting.

Here are the verses:

WHO'S WHO IN AS-IT-IS?

This newspaper would like to know who are the best and most useful citizens in the city.

Everybody think and everybody vote!

Who are the noblest folks you know,
Men and women, high and low?
Who are the pleasantest people you meet,
Who scatter sunshine along the street?

Who are the folks of kindest heart,
You meet in the club or in the mart?
Who are the finest folks there be,
In love and generosity?

Of all the city's varied host,
Who are the ones you'd miss the most?

Who are the Who-est Who's you know?
Write their names on the lines below.

Some wanted to vote for themselves, but as each had
to sign his name, no one dared to do that.

Most people voted honestly. It was very interesting
to read the lists as they came in. Mrs. Money-maker
said she just must vote for Mrs. Good-Neighbor, she
had been so good to her boy, and Mr. Money-Maker
said he was going to put down the name of Mr. Quick-
Figure, for nobody else would vote for him, and he
was a really good fellow. Mr. Big-House said the
mason ought to have a vote, for he built him so good a
house. Mrs. Late-Style wrote down the name of Mrs.
Swift-Needle, because she was "such a good soul."
When Mrs. Up-to-Date got down to the last line she
said, "I am going to vote for Mrs. Good-Taste, and I
shall tell her so."

The next week the paper contained an item that
made everybody on the hill almost forget the contest.
It said that Mr. and Mrs. Friend-o'-Man, "our distinguished newcomers," were soon to give a great reception to the four hundred best people of the city.
Invitations were soon to be issued. It would be a most
unusual and wonderful event. Nothing of the kind had
ever been known in the history of the city.

But as the days passed and no invitations arrived,
people began to wonder when the party was to be,
and who would be there.

"I am dying to know!" said Mrs. Up-to-Date one
afternoon to her friend Mrs. Late-Style.

That very evening the paper contained this item:
"Invitations have been issued today by Mr. and Mrs.

Friend-o'-Man for the reception in their new home. The city's four hundred best people are invited.

What a ringing of telephones there was in certain houses that evening!

"Have you received your invitation?"

"No, not yet."

What a ringing of telephones there was in certain houses for several days as the day of the party approached and no invitations arrived.

"Well, it's a mystery to me," said Miss High-Brow.

"It's a very great mystery to me," said Mrs. Fortunate, "and I cannot solve it."

It was a mystery, surely, but in time it cleared. On the evening of the party the paper explained it. There was an article on the first page:

"WHO'S WHO IN AS-IT-IS!

"Results of our unique voting contest.

"Citizens themselves select four hundred best people. Mr. and Mrs. Friend-o'-Man invite to their party those selected in the contest. Full list to be published tomorrow."

Then came the party. And what a party it was! Nearly all the four hundred named in the contest were there. Some had dress suits and some had not. Some had evening gowns and some had not. Everyone had on his best and his best was good enough. Everybody was friendly and kind, and so everybody was happy. They had music and games, ice cream and cake and many delicious things. The finest people were there, and the pleasantest people, and the most faithful people, and the bravest people, and the kindest people. Some lived on the hill and some lived in the valley, and some, like Mr. Friend-o'-Man, lived in between. The newspaper called it a very democratic party.

Of course, there was great indignation among the people who lived on the hill who had not been invited. They said many horrid things about Mr. and Mrs. Friend-o'-Man. But when they found out how the guests were chosen, and that they, themselves had really helped to select them, they could not, of course blame Mr. and Mrs. Friend-o'-Man, and their indignation changed to great disappointment.

The party was so successful, and everybody was so glad to honor those who had been chosen as the really best people of the city, that many similar parties were given.

Before long the term "the best people" came to have a new meaning in the city. It no longer meant the people who had the most money or the best clothes or the biggest houses, or the most servants or the greatest advantages. It meant those who were the best in character.

Discussion. How shall we choose our friends? By their clothes? The houses they live in? Or by their goodness, their kindness, their love of beautiful things, etc.?

LEADER: Mr. Edwin Markham is one of our great American poets. Years ago he saw a picture painted by Millet called "The Man With the Hoe." It made Mr. Markham think of all the people who work so hard that other people may have food to eat and clothes to wear and things to enjoy. So he wrote a poem about it that made many people think of the man with the hoe. Mr. Markham wrote another poem about friendship, especially about how he wanted to choose his friends. It says:

> Shine on me, Secret Splendor, till I feel
> That all are one upon the human wheel:
> Let me be brother to the meanest clod,
> Knowing he, too, bears on the dream of God;
> Yet, be fastidious, and have such friends,
> That when I think on them, my soul ascends![8]

LEADER: Miss Dodge must have been this kind of friend, must she not? And Jane Addams? When their friends thought of them, they must have felt happy and as though it was easy to be good. Do you remember the poem we read last week? It had a prayer at the very end, do you remember?

LEADER: (Poem. Read together again, pausing on the last line, "God make me worthy of my friends.")

Prayer. We thank thee for the gift of friendship, that makes people care for one another, for the power of love that drives out that which is greedy and mean in human hearts.

We thank thee for those who make our lives happy. May we give them comradeship and love in return. Keep us from being fickle, and make us dependable and loyal.

Guide us in our friendships that we may choose high-minded and worthy companions, whose associations will make us better men and women, and who

[8] From *Shoes of Happiness*, by Edwin Markham, Doubleday, Doran & Company, 1919, page 103. Used by permission of Mr. Virgil Markham.

will be our lifelong friends. Above all, we want Thee
as our close companion through life.[9]

THIRD SERVICE OF WORSHIP

Prelude

Hymn. "O Father, Thou Who Givest All"

Opening Sentences

LEADER: We are following the trail of being friends.
Let us think for a moment of some of the friendly
people we have met along the trail.

Silence

LEADER: Let us think of some of the people who needed
our friendship. If we were friendly, let us be happy.
If we were too busy, or forgot, or were thinking only
of ourselves—let us resolve to be more friendly this
week.

Silence

IN UNISON : Since I have no gold to give,
      And love alone must make amends,
      My only prayer is, while I live—
      God make me worthy of my friends!
      Amen.[10]

Prayer (See previous service)

Story. "The Church of the Friendly Heart."[11]

The city of Is-To-Be was like most cities of its size.
It was no better, no worse. Part of it was built on a

[9] From *A Boy's Book of Prayers* by Robert Merrill Bartlett.
Copyright, the Pilgrim Press, 1930. Used by permission.
[10] By Frank D. Sherman, in *American Student Hymnal.*
[11] By Jay T. Stocking, From *Mr. Friend-o'-Man.*

beautiful hill. There were large fine houses, shady lawns, gay flowers, clean, broad streets bordered by trees. Part of the city was in the valley. The houses in the valley were small and crowded close together. Tall chimneys of the factories stained them with smoke and dropped cinders upon them. There were no lawns, no flowers, no trees. The streets were narrow.

There were white people and black people, native people and foreign people, happy people and sad people, the same as you will find in any city.

One day workmen began to build a house halfway between the hill where the rich people lived and the valley where the poor people lived. It was such an attractive and wonderful house that people talked much about it and about the man who was coming to live in it. From time to time they gathered in little groups and discussed the stranger.

As the time drew near when the house should be finished, and the stranger should arrive in town, people talked more and more about the wonderful man who was coming from the strange Distant Land to live with them. They could hardly wait to see him.

"What's his name? Does anybody know?" they asked.

"Mr. Friend-o'-Man, I believe," said one. "I heard somebody call him that."

"It's a strange name, isn't it? I wonder how he came to have it?"

"They say he is a great churchman."

Then, as the group would break up, each would say to himself, "I hope he will go to our church."

At length the day came when the word went around among the excited people: "The stranger has come! Mr. Friend-o'-Man has come!"

People in large numbers walked past the house to see for themselves if it were really true. Sure enough, there he was! Indeed, they were all there, Mr. Friend-o'-Man, Mrs. Friend-o'-Man and all the little Friend-o'-Mans. A reporter from the city newspaper came to talk with him and ask him questions.

"I hope you will like our city," said the reporter.

"I expect to do so," said Mr. Friend-o'-Man.

"By the way," said the reporter as he rose to go, "tomorrow is Sunday. I suppose you are planning to attend some church in our city?"

"Of course I am planning to," said Mr. Friend-o'-Man.

"May I ask which one?"

"The finest church in town. It is the Church of the Friendly Heart. I heard in my distant home that it is:

> The Finest Church in Town
> The walls are built of friendly stones,
>   The friendliest to be had;
> The pews are built of friendly wood,
>   To make the stranger glad."

"I do not know that church," said the reporter.

"I do not know myself which one it is," said Mr. Friend-o'-Man, "but tomorrow I shall start out to find it."

When the newspaper was printed that evening, everybody could read in big headlines:

MR. FRIEND-O'-MAN ARRIVES

A Stranger from a Strange Country

He Is Pleased with the Town

Will Attend the Finest Church in Town

There was great excitement in every church circle. "I wonder," said many a person in the city, "if he will attend our church. I am sure I hope so."

Next morning, at the proper hour, Mr. Friend-o'-Man set out to discover the church he was looking for He addressed a man in a grand carriage.

"I am a stranger here, sir. Can you tell me which is the finest church in town?"

"Certainly, sir!" said the man gravely. "It is the Beautiful Church on the Hill. The best people in town go there. We attend that church. I am sure you will like it."

He gave very careful directions for finding it, and in a few moments Mr. Friend-o'-Man arrived at the Beautiful Church on the Hill. As he stepped inside, the ushers looked at him inquiringly. He was well dressed, of course, and of distinguished bearing. Some of them wondered whether he might be the famous stranger, but no one was sure.

"Which is your pew, please?" asked the usher politely.

"I have no pew. I am a stranger."

"Stand here awhile, please," said the usher, in a

businesslike voice, "and I'll see what I can do for you."

Some minutes later the usher beckoned to him and led him down the aisle. They stopped at a pew in which two persons were already seated. For a moment they did not move. Then they moved just enough to let the stranger pass. But it was plain that they were annoyed and did not wish to make him welcome.

Soon the service began. It was very beautiful, like the beautiful church, but Mr. Friend-o'-Man was not happy. He was too noble and proud a man, of course, to have his feelings hurt; but while they sang a hymn, he could not help thinking of the lines:

> The walls are built of friendly stones,
>   The friendliest to be had;
> The pews are built of friendly wood,
>   To make the stranger glad.

"These pews," thought he, "are surely not made of very friendly wood. This cannot be the finest church in town."

Next Sunday morning came, and Mr. Friend-o'-Man, clad in his best, once more started for church. He had not gone far before he met a man and said to him, "I am a stranger here, sir. Can you tell me which is the finest church in town?"

"Most certainly," replied the man. "It is the Big Church at the Center. The finest people in the city go there. I go there. I shall be glad to show you the way."

Very soon Mr. Friend-o'-Man found himself at the door of the Big Church. It had beautiful walls, fine windows, attractive pews. A friendly usher led him down the aisle to a pew where friendly people welcomed him. The service was helpful, and Mr. Friend-o'-Man thought he had certainly found the finest church in town.

But he wanted to make one more trial. So, a week later, instead of clothing himself in his best, he clothed himself in his worst.

When he reached the Big Church at the Center, the ushers did not recognize him. They bowed rather stiffly, and one of them waved his hand toward a seat. Mr. Friend-o'-Man started down the aisle to the seat he had occupied the Sunday before, when an usher plucked his sleeve and showed him to a pew at one side, where sat several other men who were poorly clad. The service was good, but all the while Mr. Friend-o'-Man kept thinking,

> The aisles are made, the carpets laid,
> For poor men's feet to tread.

"These aisles," he thought, "were surely not made for poor men's feet to tread."

He was almost discouraged, but he resolved to try once more. This time he did not wait for Sunday to come.

He went down in the valley where the poor people lived. He stopped a policeman on his beat.

"Can you tell me which is the finest church in town?"

"Oh," replied the officer, "they are all good. It depends upon what kind of a church you want. As for myself, I think the Church Around the Corner is the finest church in town."

"Why so?" asked Mr. Friend-o'-Man.

"Well," said the policeman, "it is full of friendly folks. They always speak to me, and they are kind and helpful to those in trouble."

"What is the name of the church?" asked Mr. Friend-o'-Man.

"I don't know its real name; I call it the Church of the Friendly Heart."

A little farther on Mr. Friend-o'-Man stopped a postman.

"Can you tell me," he asked, "which is the finest church in town?"

"Oh, every man to his taste. As for me, I like the Church Around the Corner better than any other."

"Why so?" asked Mr. Friend-o'-Man.

"Well, sir, they are good folks who go there. Last winter, when the days were very cold, they often stopped me as I passed by, to offer me a bite to eat and something hot to drink."

"And what's the name of the church?" asked Mr. Friend-o'-Man.

"I'm sure I don't know the name, sir. I call it the Church of the Friendly Heart."

Mr. Friend-o'-Man spoke to the ashman just as he set a barrel down.

"Can you tell me which is the finest church in town?"

"I can; that is, I can tell you the one I call the best; it's the Church Around the Corner."

"Why do you call it the best?" asked Mr. Friend-o'-Man.

"Well, sir, they are folks with a heart who go there. They speak to me kindly and inquire about my family, and when my wife was sick, last year, the ladies came to see her."

"What's the name of the church?" asked Mr. Friend-o'-Man.

"I don't know that, sir; I think it ought to be called the Church of the Friendly Heart."

On the next street Mr. Friend-o'-Man met a small boy. His clothes were patched but clean. "My boy," said Mr. Friend-o'-Man, "can you tell me which is the finest church around here?"

"Sure," came the answer. "The Church Around the Corner; it's the best. I go there. We have a good time and lots of fun, and nobody looks at your clothes."

"What is the name of the church?"

"I don't know it's real name, but my mother says it's the Church of the Friendly Heart."

When the next Sunday came, Mr. Friend-o'-Man started straight for the Church Around the Corner. It was not beautiful, like the Church on the Hill; it was not so big as the Church in the Center, nor were there so many people attending it, but it was full of friendly folk. People with good clothes and poor clothes sat side by side. Nobody was haughty or unpleasant or spoke unkindly. Everybody was happy.

"I hope you will come again, said the minister to Mr. Friend-o'-Man as he stopped to say good-by at the close of Sunday school.

"I shall," replied Mr. Friend-o'-Man. "In fact, I shall come here all the time."

LEADER: I wonder if Mr. Friend-o'-Man had been asked to describe the church he was looking for, if he would have done it something like this. Read from the blackboard in unison:

The Church of the Living God

This is the church of my dreams;
The church of the warm heart,
Of the open mind,
Of the adventurous spirit;
The church that cares,
That heals hurt lives,
That challenges youth;
A working church,
A worshiping church,
A church of courage,
A friendly church for all people,
The church of the living God.[12]

Hymn. "O Brother Man, Fold to Thy Heart Thy Brother" (verses 1 and 2)

O brother man, fold to thy heart thy brother;
Where pity dwells, the peace of God is there;
To worship rightly is to love each other,
Each smile a hymn, each kindly deed a prayer.

Follow with rev'rent steps the great example
Of him whose holy work was "doing good";
So shall the wide earth seem our Father's temple,
Each loving life a psalm of gratitude.[13]

Before signing this hymn, read it together and talk about it. The leader might ask, "Why do you think Mr. Friend-o'-Man could worship better in the Church of the Friendly Heart?"

[12] From *World Call.*
[13] By John Greenleaf Whittier.

To worship rightly is to love each other,
Each smile a hymn, each kindly deed a prayer.

If the group seems ready for the idea, the leader may suggest that they might like to take as their motto for the year: "The Church of the Friendly Heart."

Making plans:

How shall we start? Possible suggestions:

1. Being friendly to all in our department. Shall **we** stop there?

2. Making our homes friendly.

3. Being friendly in school, to new pupils, pupils of other races, handicapped boys and girls, old people.

4. Talking over our plan with the pastor. Telling him we want our church to be known as "The Church of the Friendly Heart."

5. Making friendship posters to put up in our room to remind us of our part.

6. Sharing our plans with God in our worship services.

7. Composing a Friendship Code.

Questions to think about between now and next Sunday:

How did the church get started?
Was it a friendly church back in those early days?
Where did the church get its idea of being friendly?
What can we do to make our church a friendly church?

The leader may suggest that she will try to answer the first two of these questions next Sunday, and that she will call on the boys and girls for their ideas about the third and fourth questions.

FOURTH SERVICE OF WORSHIP

Quiet Music. Pictures of Jesus helping people may suggest to the group where the church got its ideal of friendliness.

Discussion. This service may commence with a discussion of some of the questions about which the boys and girls have been thinking.

Hymn. "At Work Beside His Father's Bench"

> At work beside his father's bench,
> At play when work was done,
> In quiet Galilee he lived,
> The friend of every one.
>
> And as he grew to be a man
> He wandered far and wide,
> To be a friend to all in need
> Throughout the country side.[14]

Story. "The Church's Birthday" by Hulda Niebuhr [15]

After this study of the beginnings of the early church, the children may like to recall and repeat together the statement about "The Church of the Living God" which they read on the preceding Sunday. The leader may suggest that they make this their prayer for their own church. The hymn "O Brother Man, Fold to Thy Heart Thy Brother" will give further opportunity for the expression of the desire to make their church a "Church of the Friendly Heart."

[14] By Alice M. Pullen, in *Beacon Song and Service Book*, No. 285. Also found in other hymnals.
[15] From *Greatness Passing By,* Charles Scribner's Sons, 1931.

FIFTH SERVICE OF WORSHIP

If the leader has suggested the possibility that the group might plan and prepare a worship service using hymns and other worship materials of the early Christian church, one Sunday might be spent in interpretation of these materials. The stories listed below may be used, the hymns read and discussed, the music played and interpreted, a vivid picture presented of a group of early Christians meeting to read Jesus' sayings [16] and a tentative worship service outlined on the blackboard. This plan may include inviting an adult group or parents or some other group in the church school to share the worship service with the juniors. The worship service might take form somewhat as follows:

Prelude and Call to Worship. Theme, "Palestrina."

PALESTRINA

Response (sung in unison). "Alleluia" from "Palestrina."

Hymn. "Adeste Fidelis" or "Come, Ye Faithful, Raise the Strain," by John of Damascus, about 750 A. D.

SPOKESMAN: (A statement about how Peter told the stories of Jesus and how Mark and Matthew and Luke wrote the sayings of Jesus so they would not be forgotten.)

[16] See Additional Worship Materials on page 84.

READER: (The Beatitudes.) (See the arrangement in *Jesus As Teacher,* by Henry Sharman.[17])

SPOKESMAN: (Statement about early pictures of Jesus in the Catacombs, as the "Good Shepherd.")

READER:
I am the good Shepherd.
The Good Shepherd giveth his life for the sheep.
Blessed are they which are persecuted for righteousness' sake, for theirs is the kingdom of heaven.
These things have I spoken unto you that in me ye might have peace. In the world ye shall have tribulation; but be of good cheer; I have overcome the world.
SPOKESMAN: (Statement about the friendliness of Jesus and of the early church.)
READER: (Parable of the Good Samaritan, one of the stories which Jesus told about friendliness. His followers remembered this story and wrote it down.)
SPOKESMAN: The early Christians remembered and prayed the prayer which Jesus taught them.

The Lord's Prayer (In unison)

Response. "Alleluia" from "Palestrina"

Story. "St. Francis of Assisi" (Optional)

Hymn. "All Creatures of Our God and King." The words are by St. Francis of Assisi, 1225 A. D.

LEADER: (A statement regarding the resolve of this group to be friendly like Jesus and St. Francis and the early Christian community.)

Union Repetition. "The Church of the Living God"

17 Harper & Brothers, 1935.

ADDITIONAL WORSHIP MATERIALS

SOME EARLY CHRISTIAN WORSHIP MATERIALS

Hymns (found in most church hymnals)

"Now with Creation's Morning Song," by Aurelius Clemens Prudentius, 348-414 A. D.

"O Splendor of God's Glory Bright," by Ambrose of Milan, 340-397 A. D.

"Shepherd of Tender Youth," Clement of Alexandria, 220 A. D.

During the persecution of the Christians in Rome they often held their secret meetings in the Catacombs, where they had buried their dead ones. "He (Jesus) made his followers think of God in the new and lovely way of a very human Father, and of himself as the Beautiful Shepherd. The commentary supplied by those remaining frescoes in the Catacombs which are of the apostolic and sub-apostolic era, give us the same impression. Painted by torchlight in the gloom of these confined and terrifying chambers, . . . they are funereal; yet they bring the light of the gay life above—birds and flowers, garlands and landscapes—down to the chambers of the dead. There is indeed no thought of death, and hardly a sign that many who lay there had met the death of martyrs. The tiny chapels, made only for memorial purposes, are so gaily decorated that were their white plaster and bright wreaths copied in a modern church the congregation would say 'They have made our church look like a theatre.' There exist 'three pictures of the Good—the Beautiful—Shepherd, always a fair beardless youth, dressed as a shepherd of the

Campagna, in a short tunic, sometimes with a staff, and sometimes playing upon pipes.' "[18]

Responses

The "Gloria Patri."
Selections from Palestrina.

Stories

1. *The Story Peter Told*, by Elsie Ball (Henry Holt & Co.), Chapters I and XXVI. The story of the beginnings of the early church and the writing down of the records of Jesus' life and teachings.

2. "Marius Meets the Christians"[19]

It was a bright spring morning when Marius left his beautiful home in the hill country of Italy to ride to Rome for a holiday. Marius was very much excited over this trip, for he had never been to Rome. It was called "The Golden City," and Marius had dreamed of some day seeing its marble buildings, its great forum with temples to the Roman gods and its theatre where the gladiatorial contests were held.

It was at noon, when he stopped at an inn to rest, that he looked up and saw Cornelius standing there in his shining armor and knew the moment that he l

[18] From *Christianity and Art* by Pearcy Dearm
Press, 1926, pages 10 and 11.
[19] From material in *Marius the Epicurean,*
The Macmillan Company, 1929.

at him that he had found a new friend. Cornelius was a captain in the emperor's guard and they traveled the rest of the way together.

In the days that followed, the friendship of these two young men grew. Cornelius showed Marius all over Rome. Rome may have been called the "Golden City" but it was a wicked city, too, Marius discovered. Rich people rode by in gorgeous litters carried by slaves whose lives were often very hard. The poor people, on every side, were dying of the plague, brought back by the soldiers from the wars. There were shrines to the many gods on almost every street corner, for the people of Rome were superstitious. Marius could see mothers carrying their sick children up the steps of the temples in the hope that, by merely touching the statue of the god, their children might be healed.

One thing Marius noticed about his new friend, Cornelius. He turned away from all the temples. He did not spend his money going to the gladiatorial shows, where animals, and sometimes human beings, were treated cruelly. He did not sit around in the wine shops with other soldiers of the emperor's guards. In the midst of all the wickedness of the city Cornelius walked, taking no part in it. He always seemed to possess some inner secret that made him very happy. Marius wished that he might know what was Cornelius' secret of happiness. What made it easy for him to be good in the midst of so much badness? And kind when others took cruelty for granted?

Then one evening Marius discovered the secret. He and Cornelius were returning to Rome from a trip country. When they were still two miles from the city, just at sunset, Cornelius stopped at a doorway in a long wall along the public road. The doorway opened into the courtyard of a house set against a rocky hill. The moment they stepped into the courtyard Marius heard in the distance the singing of children's voices, singing with a wonderful sort of happiness.

Across the courtyard they went, through the house, and out again into a garden; then across the garden to a small door opening into the very side of the hill. When the door closed behind them, Marius found that they were in one of the Catacombs, the underground burial place of the Christians, many of whom had been killed as martyrs. But there was no sadness here, for on all the walls were pictures in gay and lovely colors, some of the Good Shepherd; others of people whose faces were full of joy, for they believed that death could not kill the human soul.

At the end of the Catacombs they came out into a large room where the children were singing. But there were old and young, rich and poor together, and every once in a while they would all sing their joyful song," "Hail! Heavenly Light!" It seemed they were celebrating the birthday of one named Jesus, one whose life had been wonderful and whose teachings they were trying to follow. Cornelius explained this to Marius. And now Marius knew what it was that made Cornelius so different from other Roman young men; now Marius began to see why Cornelius was filled with an inner happiness. He was one of these Christians who met in secret to remember the words of Jesus, such words as: "Fear not. Your Heavenly Father cares for you." "You are the light of the world." "Let your light so shine before men that they may see your good works and glorify your Father who is in heaven."

All through the service that morning, as Marius looked into the faces of those Christians, so full of hope and joy; as he listened to the singing of the children, there was in Marius' heart the beginning of a new hope. Might he, too, like his friend, Cornelius, be one of these Christians and have them for his friends?

3. "St. Francis of Assisi"

The dark blue sky of an Italian night was studded with sparkling stars that seemed to be twinkling with laughter at the pranks of a lively group of gay young fellows as they came out from a house halfway up the steep street of the little city of Assisi.

As they strayed together down the street they sang the love-songs of their country, and then a rich, strong voice rang out singing a song in French.

"That is Francis Bernardone," one neighbor would say to another, nodding his head, for Francis could sing, not only in his native Italian, but also in French.

"He lives like a prince; yet he is but the son of a cloth merchant—rich though the merchant be."

So the neighbors, we are told, were always grumbling about Francis, the wild spendthrift. For young Francis dressed in silk and always in the latest fashion; he threw his pocket-money about with a free hand. He loved beautiful things. He was very sensitive. He would ride a long way round to avoid seeing the dreadful face of a poor leper, and would hold his nose in his cloak as he passed the place where the lepers lived.

He was handsome in face, gallant in bearing, idle and careless; a jolly companion, with beautiful courtly manners. His dark chestnut hair curled over his smooth, rather small forehead. His black twinkling eyes looked out under level brows; his nose was straight and finely shaped.

When he laughed he showed even, white, closely set teeth between thin sensitive lips. He wore a short, black beard. His arms were shortish; his fingers long and sensitive. He was lightly built; his skin was delicate.

He was witty, and his voice when he spoke was powerful and sonorous, yet sweet-toned and very clear.

For him to be a son of a merchant seemed to the gossips of Assisi all wrong—as though a gray goose had hatched out a gorgeous peacock.

The song of the revelers passed down the street and died away. The little city of Assisi slept in quietness on the slopes of the Apennine Mountains under the dark clear sky.

A few nights later, however, no song of any revelers was heard. Francis Bernardone was very ill with a fever. For week after week his mother nursed him; and each night hardly believed that her son would live to see the light of the next morning. When at last the fever left him, he was so feeble that for weeks he could not rise from his bed. Gradually, however, he got better; as he did so the thing that he desired most of all in the world was to see the lovely country around Assisi— the mountains, the Umbrian Plain beneath, the blue skies, the dainty flowers.

At last one day, with aching limbs and in great feebleness, he crept out of doors. There were the great Apennine Mountains on the side of which his city of Assisi was built. There were the grand rocky peaks pointing to the intense blue sky. There was the steep street with the houses built of stone of a strange delicate pink color, as though the light of dawn were always on them. There were the dark green olive trees, and the lovely tendrils of the vines. The gay Italian flowers were blooming.

Stretching away in the distance was one of the most beautiful landscapes of the world; the broad Umbrian Plain with its browns and greens melting in the distance into a bluish haze that softened the lines of the distant hills.

How he had looked forward to seeing it all, to being in the sunshine, to feeling the breeze on his hot brow! But what—he wondered—had happened to him? He looked at it all, but he felt no joy. It all seemed dead and empty. He turned his back on it and crawled indoors again, sad and sick at heart. He was sure that he would never feel again "the wild joys of living."

As Francis went back to his bed he began to think what he should do with the rest of his life. He made up his mind not to waste it any longer; but he did not see clearly what he should do with it.

A short time after, Francis begged a young nobleman of Assisi, who was just starting to fight in a war, if he might go with him. The nobleman—Walter of Brienne, agreed; so Francis bought splendid trappings for his horse, and a shield, sword and spear. His armor and his horse's harness were more splendid than even those of Walter. So they went clattering together out of Assisi.

But he had not gone thirty miles before he was smitten again by fever. After sunset one evening he lay dreamily on his bed when he seemed to hear a voice.

"Francis," it asked, "what could benefit thee most, the master or the servant, the rich man or the poor?"

"Why, then," went on the voice, "dost thou leave God, Who is the Master and rich, for man, who is the servant and poor?"

"Then, Lord, what will Thou that I do?" asked Francis.

"Return to thy native town, and it shall be shown thee there what thou shall do," said the voice.

"He obediently rose and went back to Assisi. He tried to join again in the old revels, but the joy was gone. He went quietly away to a cave on the mountainside and there he lay—as young Mahomet had done, you remember, five centuries before, to wonder what he was to do.

Then a vision came to him. All at once like a flash his mind was clear, and his soul was full of joy. He saw the love of Jesus Christ—who had lived and suffered and died for love of him and of all men; that love was to rule his own life! He had found his Captain—the Master of his life, the Lord of his service—Christ.

Yet even now he hardly knew what to do. He went home and told his friends as well as he could of the change in his heart.

Some smiled rather pityingly and went away saying to one another: "Poor fellow; a little mad, you can see; very sad for his parents!"

Others simply laughed and mocked.

One day, very lonely and sad at heart, he clambered up the mountainside to an old church just falling into

ruin near which, in a cavern, lived a priest. He went
into the ruin and fell on his knees.

"Francis," a voice in his soul seemed to say, "dost
thou see my house going to ruin? Buckle to and
repair it."

He dashed home, saddled his horse, loaded it with
rich garments and rode off to another town to sell the
goods. He sold the horse too; trudged back up the hill,
and gave the fat purse to the priest.

"No," said the priest, "I dare not take it unless your
father says I may."

But his father, who had got rumor of what was
going on, came with a band of friends to drag Francis
home. Francis fled through the woods to a secret cave,
where he lay hidden till at last he made up his mind to
face all. He came out and walked straight toward home.
Soon the townsmen of Assisi caught sight of him.

"A madman," they yelled, throwing stones and sticks
at him. All the boys of Assisi came out and hooted and
threw pebbles.

His father heard the riot and rushed out to join the
fun. Imagine his horror when he found that it was his
own son. He yelled with rage, dashed at him and,
clutching him by the robe, dragged him along, beating
and cursing him. When he got him home, he locked
him up. But some days later Francis' mother let him
out, when his father was absent; and Francis climbed
the hill to the church.

The bishop called in Francis and his father to his
court to settle the quarrel.

"You must give back your father all that you have,"
he said.

"I will," replied Francis.

He took off all his rich garments and put the clothes and the purse of money at his father's feet.

"Now," he cried, "I have but one father. Henceforth I can say in all truth 'Our Father Who art in heaven.'"

A peasant's cloak was given to Francis. He went thus, without home or any money, a wanderer. He went to a monastery and slaved in the kitchen. A friend gave him a tunic, some shoes, and a stick. He went out wandering in Italy again. He loved everybody; he owned nothing; he wanted everyone to know the love of Jesus as he knew and enjoyed that love.

There came to Francis many adventures. He was full of joy; he sang even to the birds in the woods. Many men joined him as his disciples in the way of obedience, of poverty and of love. Men in Italy, in Spain, in Germany and in Britain caught fire from the flame of his simple love and careless courage. Never had Europe seen so clear a vision of the love of Jesus. His followers were called the Lesser Brothers (Friars Minor).[20]

[20] Basil Mathews, *Book of Missionary Heroes*, Harper & Brothers, 1922.

4

JESUS

"Why does he make our hearts so strangely still,
Why stands he forth so stately and so tall?
Because he has no self to serve, no will
That works against the well-fare of the All."[1]

It is the unique contribution of great religious leaders to touch life with a new quality, to give it deeper and richer meanings for all those who come in contact with them. The creative quality of the life of Jesus stands out clearly through the old records and has persisted down through the centuries. In spite of uncertainties and confusions in these records, the ability of Jesus to bring a more abundant life to all who knew him is evident; and we have the testimonies of countless readers of the records down the years to this creative quickening in their own lives as they have sought to understand the deep significance of his teaching and of his approach to God and to people.

There are limitations of experience and of background which make a complete appreciation of the significance of Jesus' life impossible without the study which may come with mature years. But some understanding of the things for which he stood and lived and gave his life is essential and possible for boys and

[1] "Christus," from *New Poems, Eighty Songs at Eighty*, by Edwin Markham, Doubleday Doran & Company, 1932, page 6. Used by permission of Mr. Virgil Markham.

girls. This understanding should be a meaningful part of their religious heritage.

Charles Hanson Towne, with the insight of the poet, has caught for us this value in the life of Jesus, when he writes,

> Had He not breathed His breath
> Truly at Nazareth;
> Had not His very feet
> Roamed many a hill and street;
> Had Mary's story gone
> To Time's oblivion;
> Had the sweet record paled
> And the truth not prevailed;
> Dormant and bleak had been
> This transitory scene,
> And dark, thrice dark our earth
> Unknowing of His birth.
>
> The flowers beheld His face,
> The stars knew His white grace,
> The grass was greener for
> His humble stable door;
> The rose upon its stem
> Redder for Bethlehem.
> And we—are we not wise
> To cling with avid eyes
> To the old tale, and be
> Moved by its memory?
> Unutterably dim
> Our bright world, lacking him.[2]

The full impact of Jesus' life and teaching cannot be conveyed in any one series of worship services. This

[2] "The Deathless Tale," by Charles Hamson Towne, *Ladies' Home Journal*, 1929, Curtis Publishing Co.

must be accomplished through the teaching of his life in the regular units of study in the church-school curriculum. But through worship some glimpses may be had into his sources of power, the motives which inspired his living and teaching and the results of the impact of his life upon the life and thought of the world.

Some such series as this might well precede the celebration of Christmas in the church school, to suggest why the world celebrates the birthday of Jesus—a day too often associated merely with the legendary place and circumstances of Jesus' birth. When we celebrate the birthdays of any great persons, such as Washington, Lincoln, Livingston, Pasteur, we recall and try to make dramatic the unique contributions of the personality whose birthday it is. The important thing about Abraham Lincoln does not happen to be the log cabin in which he chanced to be born. Few, in thinking of Jane Addams, give more than a passing thought to the Illinois town of her birth; instead we identify her with Hull House and the great city of Chicago into whose life she so generously poured her own. How many associate with Louisa May Alcott the Philadelphia suburb in which she was born? On the other hand the name "Louisa Alcott" spells Concord and Boston where she lived and did her work. What grips us about any outstanding life is what this life has stood for and accomplished; how this personality has changed the attitudes and ideas of people down the years; the social heritage which it has left in which we may all rejoice.

As boys and girls grow toward maturity the significant thing about the birth of Jesus should not be the manger in a stable, but the hills and waysides and homes of Galilee and Judea where he mingled with men and women and children and changed the current of their lives.

SERVICES OF WORSHIP

FIRST SERVICE OF WORSHIP

If the story of Jesus, "Behold, This Dreamer!"[3] has been told to the group at some earlier time, the leader might commence by mentioning the story. Help the group to recall the three parts of the dream of the young Jesus. Suggest that, for the next few Sundays, we are going to read and hear some stories about Jesus. Some of these were written by his friends or by people who had met his friends and had heard the stories from them. Some have been written by people living in recent times who have read the records of Jesus so many times and have studied his teachings so carefully that they think they can imagine the kinds of things he must have said and done. The first story is one of this latter kind.

One purpose of this opening story is to present a concrete and vivid picture of Jesus and his contacts with people, so that boys and girls may understand what is meant by "bringing new life" to men. In presenting a picture of Jesus it is not the intention to emphasize the miracles of healing. On the other hand, it is desirable to suggest how new physical as well as spiritual energy can come to people who are given a

[3] See page 5, Chapter I.

purpose to live for. Some reference to modern cures, based on scientific processes, might be made.

Introductory Story

It was still dark, dark as the deepest night, when a door in the little mountain village opened, ever so softly, and a boy of twenty slipped out into the darkness. He began to climb the mountain trail that led from the sleeping village up to a high point in the hills above. In spite of the darkness he did not stumble, for morning after morning, Jesus of Nazareth had slipped out of his home before dawn to climb the hills and watch the sunrise and feel that God was near.

But, though the young Jesus climbed the hills in the early morning to be alone, he knew that when the dawn had come and he climbed down the trail again to his carpenter's shop, he would not be long alone. For Jesus was the village favorite. Somehow or other the boys and girls were forever stopping in at the little shop, to watch Jesus make the smooth oxen yokes and to hear him tell stories while he worked. But it was not only the boys and girls who liked to stop in at Jesus' shop. There was Nagi who wouldn't let his oxen wear yokes made by anyone but Jesus. "The beasts are always comfortable when they wear one of your yokes," he said to Jesus. "Let us feel how smooth they are," begged the boys who were watching and listening. So Jesus stopped his work long enough for them to run their hands over the smooth curve of the wood.

In the springtime, when the long procession of villagers started out to walk to the Feast of the Passover at Jerusalem, it was Jesus who was always surrounded by a crowd of boys, swinging along beside him, singing the songs which he started and listening at night around the campfire to the stories he told.

It never occurred to any of these boys that Jesus would ever leave Nazareth. But ten years passed by. And Jesus was gone. One morning he had closed the door of his carpenter shop behind him and had walked down the village street and away. The next thing Jesus' friends knew, word came that he was teaching great crowds in the cities beyond Nazareth. Sometimes one of his Nazareth friends would go to Capernaum on business, and when he came back, he would have great tales to tell of the things which Jesus was doing. "Why, he is even healing people," this villager would exclaim. "I, myself, with my own eyes, saw a boy who lives on a street near my aunt's house in Capernaum. He has never walked since he was a baby, but they say that one day when Jesus went by, the boy was sitting on the street in front of the house. Jesus looked at him and said, 'From this time on you can walk.' And the boy is running all over Capernaum, exclaiming to everyone, 'I am well; I can walk and climb; I shall be strong; I can work; I can take care of my mother and little brothers as they say Jesus did of his. All my life is new for me.' "

It may be that some of Jesus' Nazareth friends, after hearing these stories, would go in little groups to some place where the crowds were gathered around Jesus. It may be that some of them were on the hillside overlooking the Sea of Galilee that morning when Jesus was saying to the people, "Do not be anxious; your Heavenly Father cares for you." As these old friends listened to him they may have said to each other, "He is bringing new life to all these people just as he did to us when we were boys together on the hills of Nazareth."

After the telling of the story the leader might show some pictures of Jesus teaching the people. An effective picture is Burnand's "And the Common People Heard Him Gladly." Jesus is not shown, only the crowds of eager people whose faces have fallen into different expressions of listening.

LEADER. We cannot see Jesus in this picture. Instead, we are looking into the faces of the people and they are looking at Jesus. How can you tell that they are listening to every word? What do you think Jesus might be saying at this very minute?

Allow time for a number of responses. It might be well to have some of Jesus' sayings read by several of the pupils from *Jesus As Teacher,* by Dr. Sharman.

Another picture to use is Copping's "Sermon on the Mount" or William Hole's interpretation of the same scene.

LEADER. In this picture let us look into the faces of the people who are listening to Jesus. You can see that they are seated on a hillside. Probably they have come from a long distance to hear him. What do you suppose he is saying to make them listen so intently? What new thoughts is he giving them? (Scripture: "Happy are ye," Matthew 5:3-12; "Take no thought," Matthew 6:25-34)

LEADER. Do you think Jesus just suddenly got these

thoughts about God? Or do you imagine that they had been growing in his mind for a long time? Most people begin to think and to dream when they are boys and girls. Do you know some of the things which the boy Jesus saw and did in his home that may have made him think about God?

a. Three times a day the boy Jesus recited from memory the Shema.

"Hear, O Israel, the Lord our God is one Lord. And thou shalt love the Lord they God with all thine heart and with all thy soul and with all thy might."

b. On entering the house the boy Jesus and his brothers and sisters would touch the little case over the door containing the sacred words of the scripture and then reverently kiss the fingers that had touched the holy name of God. Even the baby of the family would be lifted to put his tiny hand on the mezuza.

c. At meal times, Joseph, the father, while the children listened very quietly, would say.

"Blessed art Thou, O Lord our God, King of the Universe, who hast brought forth bread from the ground."

d. Every Friday, just at nightfall, the children would wait for Joseph as he returned from the synagogue service of preparation, and watch their mother as she lighted the Sabbath lamps. Joseph would come in, and as the children stood in the dim glow of the lamps, he would bless each child.

e. There was the beautiful Feast of Dedication, when each evening one more candle was lighted in the home. On the first night one light for each member of the family, and on each succeeding night one more for each member, until on the last night the little house would be aglow with the many lights. All of these things reminded the boy Jesus that God was always near and about him. Is it any wonder that when the people said to him, "Lord, teach us to pray," he should have taught them the prayer which begins "Our Father who art in heaven"?

In the earliest records about Jesus we can read a story about this prayer which we call "The Lord's Prayer" and which is used all over the world by Christian churches wherever they meet.

Scripture Reading. Luke 11:1-10

LEADER. Though the story tells us that Jesus taught this prayer to his disciples, it is a prayer that anyone of any religion can pray. Some years ago there was a great World's Fair held in Chicago. Because there were people from all parts of the world, it was decided to hold a Congress of Religions where Jews, Christians, Mohammedans, Confucians, Buddhists could tell each other about their religions. At the opening session Dr. Barrows, the president of Oberlin College, was presiding. As he looked down into the thousands of faces of people of all races and religions, he tried to think of a prayer that they could all say together. And he said to himself, "That prayer is the Lord's Prayer; there is not a sentence in it that anyone of any religion cannot pray, no matter what he believes." So, with the help of interpreters, this great congregation of people united in saying the prayer that Jesus taught his disciples. Today, on any Sunday morning, when we in this country are saying this prayer in our churches, we may remember that Christians in churches all over the world are also repeating it in hundreds of different languages.

LEADER. Let us think about the words of this prayer as we look into the faces of these people on the hillside. What are some of the words which you think would have comforted them and have given them courage to go on living? What words in the prayer suggest a new way of living?

Prayer. The Lord's Prayer (repeated slowly and thoughtfully)

Hymn. "O Thou Great Friend to All the Sons of Men," or the following hymn, sung to the tune of "Truro"

> O rugged Master of the hills,
> The desert and the storm-swept sea,
> The earnest heart, responsive, thrills
> With each new glimpse we gain of thee.
>
> Among the fields of Palestine,
> Beneath the parching eastern blaze,
> Those eager, tireless feet of thine
> Trod joyously the crowded ways.
>
> While journeying the open road
> Thou ministered to human need,
> As Pilgrim with a staff and load,
> The friend to all in word and deed.[4]

SECOND SERVICE OF WORSHIP

In the following service of worship, before each

[4] From *Social Hymns*, A. S. Barnes & Company.

act of remembering Jesus, an appropriate picture may be shown while the group sits in silence for a few moments looking at the picture.

Opening Sentences

> Judean hills are holy,
> Judean hills are fair,
> For one can find the footprints
> Of Jesus everywhere.
> One finds them in the twilight
> Beneath the singing sky,
> Where shepherds watch in wonder
> White planets wheeling by.

Hymn. "O Rugged Master of the Hills"

LEADER: (Showing the first picture, "Hilltop at Nazareth"[5] by Elsie Anna Wood) Let us unite in an act of remembering Jesus. Let us remember the boy Jesus who, in the early morning, before the village was awake, may have climbed the hills above the little town to watch the sunrise and to feel God's presence before he began the work of the day.

Silence

LEADER: (Showing a picture of Jesus as a boy in the carpenter shop[5]) Let us remember the boy Jesus who must have pitied all tired and homeless animals; who, in his father's carpenter shop, probably learned to make yokes so smooth that no oxen, wearing them, would be hurt. Let us think of the kindness of Jesus to all living things.

Silence

LEADER: (Showing the picture "Jesus and the Chil-

[5] See Picture Source Materials, pages 119-120.

dren"[5] by Elsie Anna Wood) Let us remember the
young man Jesus in Nazareth, who worked at his
father's bench while the village boys may have crowded
around him to watch him at his work and to listen to
the stories which he told. Let us think of Jesus hiking
over the hills with these boys, watching the sunsets
with them, their friend and their comrade.

Silence

LEADER: (Showing the picture "Jesus and the Children"[5] by William Hole) Let us remember Jesus in the
crowded streets of Capernaum, or on the mountainside
or by the blue sea, telling people that they need not
worry, for God cared for them; helping people to
begin over again and live new lives. Let us think of
Jesus bringing new life to many people.

Prayer. Let the leader repeat the phrases of the Lord's
Prayer very slowly, pausing between each phrase for
a moment of quiet. The prayer might be preceded by
a brief period of conversation in which each idea in
the prayer is discussed sufficiently to be sure that its
meaning is clear. This conversation might be stimulated
by asking the group to think of experiences of Jesus
which might have made him think of each phrase.

Hymn. "O Thou Great Friend to All the Sons of
Men"

THIRD SERVICE OF WORSHIP

Some class might arrange an art exhibit of pictures of Jesus in the homes of Palestine, in the streets
of the cities, on the hillsides or by the sea, teaching and
walking along the roads with his friends. As the

boys and girls enter, let this class in charge of the exhibit act as ushers, guiding the others through the art gallery. Suggestions for pictures and picture sources are given at the close of this chapter.

Prelude. Music of the hymn, "Judean Hills Are Holy" Opening Sentences. The first verse of the hymn, read by the leader.

Hymn. "Judean Hills Are Holy."

LEADER: One of the things we like to do is to imagine what Jesus must have done when he was a boy of our age. One writer has made up a story about a trip that the boy Jesus made with his father. In the story a man in Capernaum came all the way to Nazareth to ask Joseph, the carpenter, to come to Capernaum and build a house for him. Joseph said he would do it. Then, as he began to make plans for his journey, he said to Jesus one day, "Lad, would you like to travel to Capernaum with me and help me build the new house?" Jesus was all excitement. A trip! With his father! A new city!

"Is it on the water?" he asked. "Shall I see boats and fishermen?"

"Yes," replied Joseph. "You will probably see many fishermen. Perhaps you can go out in a boat yourself."

So it happened that early one morning Joseph and Jesus said good-by to Mary, and with the little donkey, started out down the mountain trail from Nazareth. Of course the trip was exciting, for the trail wound through the mountains northward, toward the blue sea of Galilee. One night, after dark, they

Judean Hills Are Holy [6]

William L. Stidger

Gesangbuch der Herzogl, 1784
Adapted by James R. Houghton

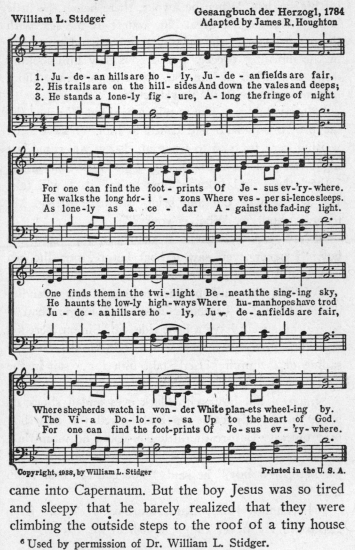

1. Ju - de - an hills are ho - ly, Ju - de - an fields are fair,
2. His trails are on the hill- sides And down the vales and deeps;
3. He stands a lone-ly fig - ure, A - long the fringe of night

For one can find the foot- prints Of Je - sus ev-'ry-where.
He walks the long hor - i - zons Where ves - per si-lence sleeps.
As lone-ly as a ce - dar A - gainst the fad-ing light.

One finds them in the twi - light Be - neath the sing-ing sky,
He haunts the low-ly high-ways Where hu-man hopes have trod
Ju - de - an hills are ho - ly, Ju - de - an fields are fair,

Where shepherds watch in won - der White plan-ets wheel-ing by.
The Vi - a Do - lo - ro - sa Up to the heart of God.
For one can find the foot-prints Of Je - sus ev - 'ry-where.

came into Capernaum. But the boy Jesus was so tired
and sleepy that he barely realized that they were
climbing the outside steps to the roof of a tiny house

[6] Used by permission of Dr. William L. Stidger.

where he fell asleep while friendly hands were slipping off his sandals. When he awoke, there below the little house stretched the great blue waters of the sea, with the many boats of the fishermen bobbing up and down in the morning breeze. Some boys saw him looking down and called to him. So, down to the sandy shore he ran to play with his new friends.

"How would you like to take a boat ride?" asked the tall brown boy who had called to him. "I have been waiting here for you to wake up. I saw you come last night but you were too sleepy to see me. This is my father's boat and I know how to sail it. I will take you a little way out and bring you back safely. My name is Andrew. What is yours?"

"I am Jesus. I came from Nazareth," said the boy. "I never even saw a boat before, nor the sea either, at least close like this."

"Well, then, you'll be sure to like it. It's splendid. There comes my brother Simon. He's bigger than I, so we can surely have a boat ride. Hi, Simon, here's a boy who never saw a lake or a boat in his life or went sailing or swimming. Let's take him for a sail in the boat."

Simon, a tall boy, with black eyes and a shock of bushy black hair came up and looked the new boy over quickly. Before the little boy could do more than smile, he cried out, "Why not? Come on, I'll steer. Sit here, new boy," he said. "You can see best from here."

"His name's Jesus," said Andrew. "He came from Nazareth. He never caught a fish in his life."

"That's nothing" said Simon, hauling at the sail. "We can teach him to fish. What can he do?"

"I'm going to help my father build a house for our kinsman, Eleazer," answered the little boy. "And I know lots of good stories and I have a knife which Baruch, the peddler, got in Damascus."

"I like you," cried Simon, throwing out a white sail. "I wish you'd stay in Capernaum always."

"I like you, too," said the new boy. "I think I will have to go back to Nazareth soon but I might come back here sometime."

. . . .

"Tell us a story," asked the boys. So Jesus told them the story of the two friends, David and Jonathan.

"Why couldn't we be friends, like that?" said impulsive Simon, laying a warm brown hand on [Jesus'] shoulder. "You and Andrew and I. Why couldn't we be?"[7]

LEADER. So this storyteller imagines that Jesus had met Andrew and his brother Simon, when they were all boys. We do not know that this is true, but it might have been. Years later, one morning Andrew and Simon were just casting their nets into the sea, when they heard a voice calling to them. Who would be calling them so early in the morning? The story has come down to us through the many years that have passed since then. Simon Peter, himself, told it to a young man, John Mark, who wrote it down word for

[7] From *The Little Boy of Nazareth* by Edna M. Bonser, Harper & Brothers, 1930.

word as Peter told it to him. This is what Simon Peter remembered as happening that morning.

Scripture. Mark 1 :14-23 (to the word "scribes") ; Mark 1 :28-38.

The picture of "Jesus and the Fishermen" by Zimmerman might be shown to accompany the scripture reading.

LEADER : As we think of Simon's story of how "in the evening after sunset, they brought to him all who were sick or possessed by demons and the whole town was gathered at the door," let us sing a hymn which tells much the same story.

Hymn. "When the Golden Evening Gathered"[8]

When the golden evening gathered
On the shore of Galilee,
When the fishing boats lay quiet by the sea,
Long ago the people wondered,
Though no sign was in the sky,
For the glory, the glory of the Lord was passing by.

Not in robes of purple splendor,
Nor in silken softness spun,
But in raiment worn with travel did he come ;
And the people knew his presence
By the heart that ceased to sigh
When the glory, the glory of the Lord was passing by.

For he healed their sick at even,
And he cured the leper's sore,
And sinful men and women sinned no more,

[8] Sung to the tune "Gosterwood," an English Traditional Melody, No. 72 in the *Beacon Song and Service Book,* Beacon Press, 1935.

And the world grew mirthful-hearted,
And forgot its misery
When the glory, the glory of the Lord was passing by.

Not in robes of purple splendor,
But in lives that do his will,
In patient acts of kindness he comes still;
And the people cry with wonder,
Though no sign is in the sky,
That the glory, the glory of the Lord is passing by.[9]

LEADER: H. and M. and G. are going to take the parts of the two fishermen brothers, James and John, and their father, Zebedee. We will imagine that it is the day after Jesus has asked them to leave their nets and follow him. They are trying to make their father understand what it is about Jesus that makes them want to give up fishing to go with him.

Dramatic Conversation. (By three older boys or three teachers. This may be read if the participants have gone over it enough times to know its content very well and have discussed its meaning and practiced interpreting it with the adult leader. A still better method would be for the boys to read and discuss the selection and then put it into their own words.)

ON THE GALILEAN LAKE[10]

JAMES AND JOHN: Father—hast thou seen Jesus?
ZEBEDEE: Nay, my sons, I have not closely seen him. Simon pointed him to me the other morn but it was too

[9] By William Dawson, found in the *American Student Hymnal,* H. Augustine Smith, Ed., D. Appleton-Century Company, 1928, page 67.
[10] By Arthur W. Moulton, from *It Came to Pass,* R. G. Badger Co., 1916.

far for me to see him well. The children of the village
were about him. Dost thou know him?

JAMES: Yea, father, somewhat, we wish we knew him
better: may we not bring him to thee?

ZEBEDEE: Certainly, my sons, but when hast thou seen
him?

JOHN: Oh, father, some of the mornings when we
could not go out upon the sea we have gone into the
village to see him.

ZEBEDEE: They say the shop is full of men who go to
see him: why, I wonder?

JAMES: Oh, father, thou shouldst go down, and speak
to him and let him speak to thee. Thou wouldst love
him, father.

ZEBEDEE: Perhaps, but my two sons fill my heart: I
love thee and am happy.

JAMES: Ay, but father, thou wouldst love him too and
thou wouldst be happy in his friendship.

ZEBEDEE: What can he bring me that my James and
John do not daily bestow upon me, ye for whom I thank
the Heavenly Father daily? Can he help me with the
trade, can he show me where the fish run larger in their
schools? Hath he thy strength?

JOHN: Oh, father, he is so strong: we saw him one
day shoulder a log which Joseph could not move, and
on the slope of Hermon only a week ago he rolled a
boulder which had blocked the trail. We sat about the
lake with him a while past and he revealed two likely
spots for fish which thou must try.

ZEBEDEE: Indeed!

JAMES: Strange worth doth cling to words he speaks.

He said the other day we ought to live our lives in bigger measure.

ZEBEDEE: What could he mean by that, my sons?

JOHN: After the measure of God, he said; that God had wonderful plans, that we ought to be builders for God and live abundantly.

ZEBEDEE: I think, my sons, in time that we shall have abundance.

JAMES: Jesus did not seem to mean that, father. He said that life in close touch with God produces a richness out of which great thoughts and deeds do spring.

ZEBEDEE: There may be truth in that, my sons.

JOHN: And he says that life is poor without that touch of God, that Nazareth and Capernaum are poor, that Jerusalem is poor because they have it not.

ZEBEDEE: Pull the boat around, my son, thou hast forgot thy task.

JAMES AND JOHN: Father, he said one day as we were sitting in his boat . . .

ZEBEDEE: Hath he a boat?

JAMES AND JOHN: Yes, one he made himself, beautiful it is, the swiftest on the lake. He said one day as we were . . .

ZEBEDEE: Can he sail the boat, my sons?

JAMES: Ah, father, thou shouldst see him sail into the storm. That very day there came a sudden storm down from the hills and caught us and he fetched us through —right head on through the gale, and all the time he smiled and said how safe the boat was and how splendid was the work of fishing and how human souls ought to be drawn into the life of faith.

ZEBEDEE: Methinks, my sons, that thou are drawn to him.

JAMES: Oh, father, no other like him hath we ever seen.

JOHN: Father, we wish to go with him.

ZEBEDEE: My sons, my sons, James, John—go with the Dreamer! Ye are beside yourselves!

JAMES: Nay, but he hath such a work to do.

ZEBEDEE: But so have ye, my sons, at home with me —ye would not leave me at my time of life, ye would not leave the fortune that is growing large—ye would not leave the home which I have built for thee—ye would not leave these days with me upon the sea—since ye were babes ye have been mine.

JOHN: Yea, father, and still we shall be thine, but since this new faith hath come to us, life seems to spring to other works; we cannot hold it to ourselves alone. It brings before our eyes the men of Galilee, the men and boys of Palestine, the multitudes within the Holy City. We want to give them this abundant treasure, strengthen their hearts and bring their souls to life.

ADDITIONAL WORSHIP MATERIALS

Stories

1. The story of Zacchaeus who learned from Jesus how to live a happy life.

2. The source for the following story is Chapter VII of *By an Unknown Disciple*,[11] a book which the leader should read for his personal enrichment before starting this series of services.

Jesus and his friends had been walking all day from

[11] *By an Unknown Disciple*, Harper & Brothers, 1919.

earliest dawn. At nightfall they came to a little village —a very poor village, where the head man greeted them and made them welcome. The man, himself, had worn clothing and in his eyes was an anxious look.

"May a blessing rest upon this house," said Jesus.

"May a blessing rest upon you. You are welcome, sir," said the woman who began at once to get the evening meal before Jesus and his friends. While she was preparing the food, Jesus watched her. He saw that she, too, looked unhappy. It was the home of a hard-working family. There was evidently very little food in the home, but the woman and her husband offered it generously.

"Have you any children?" asked Jesus.

"Yes," she replied, "they have been out with the sheep all day."

At that moment there was a noise outside and in came two tall boys and a little girl with bright eyes. The boys sat in a far corner eating their evening meal, but the little girl took her piece of bread, and after one look at Jesus, edged over toward him and leaned against his arm.

The mother started to send the little girl away, but Jesus said, "Let the child stay." The father told Jesus that many of his friends had gone to hear Jesus, but that he, himself, had been too poor. So Jesus began to talk to them, while the shadows grew deeper in the poor little room and the anxious father and mother fixed their eyes upon him while he talked. Jesus began by telling them a story.

"Once upon a time," he began, and the boys came closer so they should hear every word of the story.

(At this point let the leader open the Bible and read Jesus' story from Luke 12:16-21.)

Then Jesus, looking directly at the man said (Read Jesus' words from Luke 12:22-26). The man's eyes began to look less anxious. Then Jesus went on (Luke 12:26-30). This time, as he stopped, the man and the woman smiled at each other.

Jesus put his arm around the little girl, who had climbed into his lap and was almost fast asleep, and said, "If this child here asked you for a loaf, would you give her a stone? If you, then, being imperfect, wish to give her good gifts, will not God, who is all good, give you help when you ask it? Remember this," said Jesus (Luke 12:34).

Just then the man straightened his shoulders and stood erect as though he had found new courage to live. The woman smiled as Jesus put the sleeping child into her arms. There was a new peace in her eyes.

3. "St. Francis and the First Créche"[12]

Long, long ago there lived a man whose name was Francis. He had many friends who loved him dearly. That was not strange, for Francis was a real follower of Jesus, always finding ways of helping people to live happier and more useful lives. But he was not always happy. It made him sad when people were unkind and selfish.

One day he was very sorrowful. He was walking all alone through the woods. He had been hearing that many of his friends in the near-by village were unhappy,

[12] By Florence M. Taylor, from *The Pilgrim Elementary Teacher.* Copyright, The Pilgrim Press. Used by permission.

for they were being thoughtless of each other, and unkind and selfish. It was near Christmas time, and as Francis was walking along he was thinking of Jesus.

"If only people would really remember him!" he thought. "They couldn't keep on being selfish and unloving if only they remembered Jesus. Here it is, almost his birthday! If only somehow I could do something to make these people think about him!"

Francis walked on slowly through the woods, his head bent thoughtfully. Suddenly he looked up and smiled.

"I have it!" he cried. "That will be the very thing!"

He quickened his steps, hurrying on through the woods, until he came to the house of his friend, Giovanni, with whom he was to stay. Giovanni was very wealthy. He lived in a large house. He had many servants. Eagerly Francis told his plan, and Giovanni agreed to help.

Not far from Giovanni's house was a large grotto—a hollowed out cave in the rocks. If you had been inside the next day, you would have seen Francis working eagerly and happily. Servants of Giovanni brought in branch after branch of evergreens from the forest. Then as Francis directed, they built a little stable right there within the grotto. The air was sweet with the fragrance of the greens. When the stable was finished the floor of it was covered with straw. The servants next brought a manger filled with hay from which the animals used to eat. This Francis stood in the little stable, as though it were waiting for the coming of the little Jesus.

Still Francis had not finished. He had the men bring

in a real, live little donkey, and two white cows. They led them into the cave, and inside the stable, and there they tied them near the little manger.

The animals looked all about them. They looked at the walls of the stable. They looked out at the shadowy cave. It almost seemed as if they understood, and were glad to be part of so lovely a picture. At last Francis was satisfied.

"Go, bring in the villagers," he cried. So the servants went through the village telling everyone. "Francis, our good friend, has come. He wants us all to come to him at once. He is waiting for us."

How eagerly the people repeated the message! "Francis is here! Oh, hurry to the grotto in the hills!"

With eager haste they came crowding in. But their voices hushed as they entered. It was so beautiful they just stood and looked and looked. Something very much like this must Mary and Joseph have seen on that long-ago first Christmas Eve. How tired they must have been after their long journey! How glad to rest even in this humble place, with the gentle animals near by!

As the people from the village stood looking, happy Christmas thoughts came crowding into their hearts. They remembered Jesus and his goodness. They were ashamed of all their selfishness and unkindness. They were going to try to be better men and women. For a long while they lingered in the grotto, and Francis talked to them of Jesus and his love. Then they went slowly and quietly to their homes.

When the last one had gone, Francis knelt before the empty manger. His heart was full of joy and thankfulness. God had shown him the way to help these friends remember Jesus, and catch the true meaning of Christmas.

Scripture. In addition to the passages suggested above, consult *Jesus As Teacher*, by Henry Sharman, especially for the setting and interpretation of the Beatitudes on pages 33-38.

Suggested Pictures and Picture Sources

1. *Pictures by Elsie Anna Wood.*
   Pilgrim Press, 14 Beacon Street, Boston Massachusetts
   "The Hilltop at Nazareth"
   "Jesus and the Children"
   "Jesus Teaching from the Boat"
   "The Sermon on the Mount"
   These pictures come in a large size, as well as in the smaller sizes.
2. *Church School Closely Graded Courses.*
   Methodist Publishing House, 810 Broadway, Nashville, Tennessee; also Pilgrim Press, 14 Beacon Street, Boston, Massachusetts.

   Primary Picture Sets.

   a. *Pictures by William Hole*
      "Jesus Teaching on the Hillside"
      "He Went About Doing Good"
      "Jesus in the Home of Mary and Martha"
      "Jesus and the Children"
      "Jesus and the Fishermen"
   b. *Pictures by Harold Copping*
      "The Sermon on the Mount"

c. *Pictures Portraying Home Life and Religious Festivals in Palestine.*

Maud Tindal Atkinson, "At School in Nazareth"

Dean Cromwell, "The Carpenter of Nazareth"

William E. Fay, "We Give Thanks unto Thee" and "Springtime in Palestine"

Herman D. Giesen, "The Boy Jesus and His Friends on a Holiday" and "Boys in Palestine."

Richard A. Holberg, "A Palestinian Family"

William Hole, "And the Child Grew"

George T. Tobin, "At Home in Nazareth" and "Feast of Dedication in a Jewish Home."

3. Dr. Norman Richardson, Presbyterian Theological Seminary, Chicago, Illinois, "Thy Kingdom Come," by Signe Larson.

5

THE CHRISTMAS FESTIVAL

Christmas Prayer

"Let Christmas not become a thing
Merely of merchants' trafficking,

Of tinsel, bell and holly wreath
And surface pleasure; but beneath

The childish glamor let us find
Nourishment for soul and mind.

Let us follow kinder ways
Through the teeming human maze

And help the age of peace to come
From a dreamer's martyrdom."[1]

—MADELINE MORSE

FOR THE LEADER

The editor of one of our popular American magazines, in a Christmas message to her readers, said, "Every Christian nation has made of Christmas time something beautiful, made of the Christmas festivities something especially its own. And in every country

[1] From *Unity Magazine*.

except ours, Christmas is a strictly religious festival
—as indeed it should be." [2]

Mr. Eric Kelly, who has given us many delightful
Christmas stories with a Polish background, says of the
people of Poland and eastern Europe,

Their idea was that Christmas is not a commemorative
festival at all, but that Christ is *actually born* each Christmas Eve, and therefore a vacant place is left at the table,
and a vacant chair about the fire to be occupied by the
Christ Child if he happens to stroll in. And the Christ
Child might not come in his own self, he might come as a
stranger, the receiving of whom in His name would be the
equivalent of the reception of the actual Christ Child....

Thus I saw it in Poland. When the first Star comes on
Christmas Eve, Christ is born—not 1936 years ago, but
now—right now. And with the ringing of the doorbell, or
the knocking on the door, the presence of the Christ is
announced, and thus the children learn of the holy immi-
nence. Joy—unbounded, contagious, unabashed joy—
leaping all bounds and filling all hearts. Christ is here! The
dark past counts for naught. Markets full of toys and trees,
boys going around with puppets, and choirs carrying stars,
accordions, guitars, violins—sing, make merry, rejoice.
Christ is born and he is born in all of us. Where now is
the Puritan suspicion of evil in a heart full of joy? O
Krakow in all thy glory, thou wert never so glorious as
on this night of Christmas Eve, with the thousands below
singing a Hymn of Nativity and the great organ thunder-
ing and the trumpeters in the tower playing that wonderful
"Midst Night's Dark Shadows." [3]

These words have a poignant meaning for us in the
light of what has happened to Poland and others of

[2] By Jean Austin in the 1936 and 1938 December issues of the
American Home.

[3] From the November-December, 1936, issue of *The Horn Book*,
264 Boylston Street, Boston, Mass.

these European countries whose Christmas customs hold within themselves so many spiritual values. With worship services on the significance of the life of Jesus,[4] emphasizing the new ideas and attitudes which he aroused in people, as a background, the Christmas worship services might well suggest the rekindling in our own lives of the creative spirit with which Jesus met life. It will be natural to think about the consequent joy which people feel when they themselves are living life on a creative level or when they meet people who are doing so. The younger boys and girls may not grasp this thought fully, but they can understand that, when a creative life like that of Jesus makes such a lasting impact upon the thought of the world, it is not to be wondered at that people down the ages have built up around it beautiful legends, customs and rituals which have become traditional parts of their heritage.

The worship experiences that develop in the Christmas season ought to suggest this idea and should, further, seek to preserve the distinctly religious aspect of the Christmas festival. Through the stories of the simple peasant celebrations in many parts of the world the boys and girls may catch the reverent character of the joy attending the Christmas season.

Our American boys and girls also may be encouraged through an appreciation and practice of some of the simple religious ceremonials, such as the lighting of the Christmas candle in the window on Christmas Eve, the singing of carols, the setting up of the crèche, the attendance at Christmas Eve candlelight services, to cut themselves loose from the domination of *things* to en-

[4] See Chapter IV.

joy a simpler kind of celebration. As the editor of the
Woman's Home Companion said, "When I wish you
all a Merry Christmas, it is the simple joy and the
spiritual beauty of a peasant Christmas that I am wishing for you. May your presents be less and your happiness greater."[5]

Through appreciation of the Christmas ceremonials
of many countries may come, too, an understanding of
the universal appeal of Jesus' life to all people. There
is no more appropriate time for enjoyment of the inter-
pretations of Jesus by the artists of the world than at
Christmas time. The following poem suggests the time-
lessness as well as the universality of the Christmas
experience.

> Dear Christmas Child, no length of time nor space
> Has stayed the journey of Thy blessed feet.
> Behind no barrier of caste or race
> Have men found isolation so complete
> But that there came the shining of Thy face,—
> But that they heard Thy voice in accents sweet.
> Thus, every artist paints Thee as his own,
> Limned on the background of his time and thought;
> Set in the spaces which his life has known;
> Decked in the clothing which his hand has wrought.
> Where'er Thy seeking infant feet may roam,
> At every age and land Thou dost traverse,
> Men give Thee welcome to their hearts' best home,
> Thou little Brother of the Universe![6]

Since much of the reality of these Christmas services
will depend upon the activities out of which a genuinely
religious observance of Christmas may develop, some

[5] From the *Woman's Home Companion*, December, 1936.
[6] By Hugh L. Burleson. Source unknown.

suggestions for such activities are included at this point.

SUGGESTED ACTIVITIES TO ENRICH WORSHIP

Some of the following activities might be undertaken by different classes in the church school and the results shared in an assembly program of the entire group or in a Christmas celebration planned for the parents and other adult members of the church.

1. Visits to art galleries in communities where they are available, to see the religious paintings.

2. An appreciation study of paintings of Jesus by great artists, old and modern, each member of the group to discover the answer to the question: What artist seems to me best to interpret the character of Jesus? Include some study of the earliest known portraits of Jesus as well as some quite recent paintings.[7]

3. Begin making a collection of pictures of Jesus as a permanent collection for the church school. Plan to mount these attractively on cardboard or in a large book.

4. Make a study of the Christmas customs of different countries. Plan to share your discoveries with other groups in the church.[8]

5. Make a special study of the crèche, its origin and use in different countries.[7]

SUGGESTIONS FOR HOME ACTIVITIES

1. An out-of-door Christmas tree, not the electric-lighted tree for decorative purposes, but one in the woods (if the family lives in a village or rural environ-

[7] For helpful books, see bibliography, page 154.
[8] See *Stardust and Holly*, Dorothy Shipman, Ed., The Macmillan Company, 1932.

ment) or one in a secluded part of the yard. A family or small group (Sunday school class) celebration under the early stars, with the singing of carols and reading of Christmas poetry. Such poems as "I Do Not Like a Roof Tonight," by Grace Noll Crowell; "Oh, Bring Not Gold," by Violet Allyn Storey; "Shall I to the Byre Go Down?" by Eleanor Farjeon. Stories that suggest out-door celebrations are mentioned in the bibliography at the close of this chapter.

2. Getting out certain books and pictures reserved for the Christmas season only. Reading the life of Jesus through quickly to get the perspective of his whole life, in the weeks just preceding Christmas.

3. Setting up the crèche and associating with it stories and poetry.[7]

4. Examination of Christmas cards received in previous years as well as those coming in this year, especially those of a distinctly religious significance or those suggesting Christmas customs of different countries. Mount these very special cards in a book and make an attractive cover for it. Let the collection grow from year to year, but include only the most beautiful and religious cards. Christmas poems which are favorites with the family might also be included.

As initial preparation for this series of worship services, plan an informal period in which the Christmas customs of other countries are described.[7] Let the boys and girls be responsible for this period, perhaps the members of some class which has been making a special study of Christmas customs and traditions.

Call attention to foreign post cards which have been brought in showing such customs as peasants going to

[7] For helpful books, see bibliography, page 154.

church on Christmas Eve, the feeding of the birds in Sweden, the German cards, showing the Christ Child returning to earth on Christmas Eve, attended by the little helping-angels, bearing gifts, who visit the homes of those in need.

Such stories as the following may be told.

"Far, far off and long ago, a Russian peasant stumbling homeward through the snow conceived out of his faith a kindly habit that was destined to grow into a widespread custom. He had heard how the Virgin and Joseph vainly sought a place to rest on the first Holy Night. What if she came this night and could not find the way? What if, by chance, she found my hut? And so he placed a candle in the window—a little candle to show her the way across the snow. And so, too, he unlocked the door, so that she might come in even if the family was asleep."

Such legends as this will help the children to understand how some legends have arisen and that often the impulse which gave rise to them was one of love and kindliness.

SERVICES OF WORSHIP

FIRST SERVICE OF WORSHIP

Carol Singing. Sing some of the carols of different countries. Call attention to the customs connected with them, such as in the French carol, "Bring a Torch, Jeanette, Isabella."

Discussion. Why do we celebrate the birthdays of certain men and women? Abraham Lincoln, Jane Addams, Louisa Alcott, Louis Pasteur and others?

Why do we celebrate the birthday of Jesus? Reference may be made to the worship services in Chapter IV based on the contribution of Jesus to the life of the world.

If you were a stranger from another planet, suddenly sent to this earth and to the United States on Christmas Eve; if you were to walk through the streets of some city; if you should visit some homes and some church-school Christmas parties—what would you see that might make you think the people were celebrating a religious festival? From the possible responses of the group attempt to guide them in sorting out the observances which might impress the visitor as being of a religious nature from those which would not seem religious. These possible responses from the group might include electric lights on trees and bushes in front yards, sets of electric bulbs in windows, trees full of gifts, church services, crèches in homes and churches, stockings hung by chimneys, last-minute shopping, rushing around, wrapping gifts, postmen and shop people working late hours, baskets given to needy people, groups singing Christmas carols in the streets, some families reading Dickens' *Christmas Carol* on Christmas Eve, others reading the story of Jesus, church-school parties where a man dressed like Santa Claus gives presents to children who already have more than they need, little mention of Jesus whose birthday it is, homes stuffing turkeys and preparing puddings for Christmas dinners.

Possible comments by the leader. If our visitor from another planet had the power to fly to Europe on this same Christmas Eve, he might see many homes with windows darkened, no Christmas candle burning to light the way for the Christ Child, bombs falling, little children too afraid to sing the old carols, in some countries people not allowed to get to their churches on Christmas Eve.

And yet, before this present war, in many of these countries of Europe Christmas Eve was a time when people stopped to remember the teachings of Jesus and the life of goodness and kindness which he lived.

Shall we, during this Christmas season, make it a point to think of all these boys and girls and their fathers and mothers, in Poland, Czechoslovakia, Sweden, Norway, Finland, Germany, France, Holland, Belgium, England? Shall we look at the pictures of Jesus which the artists of these different countries have painted? Shall we sing the carols which we have learned and listen to stories of Christmas that have come to us from these countries?

A Christmas Story About Poland. "In Clean Hay" by Eric Kelly [9]

In a little village on the outskirts of the Polish city of Krakow there stands a happy farmhouse whose owner is Pan Jan. In the early spring the fields about the house are dark and rich, awaiting the planting of seed; and in the summer they are green with ripened grain. In the fall they turn to russet brown; and in the winter they lie deep beneath the shining snow. From earliest morning until sundown the house is astir with action, but at sundown everything ceases and peace

[9] From *The Christmas Nightingale*, by Eric Kelly, The Macmillan Company, 1932.

descends, for did the Lord not ordain that all work should cease with the sun? Then the lamp is lighted in the large room and the newspaper which has come from Krakow will be read to all the family by the father or the eldest boy, Antek. The others sit about and listen. Antek is fifteen and goes every day to the high school in the city; it is a walk of about three miles, but the road is good and there is often company on the way.

Antek reads from the gazette: "Tomorrow is the day before Christmas and there will be many visitors who come to the city to attend services at night in the churches. The Christmas trees will be on sale in the *Rynek* (market place) and the booths full of candy and toys will be opened directly after dark. In the homes, the children will await the sight of the first star: when the first star shines, then an angel will come and knock at the door, and the rejoicing at the birth of Christ will begin. This year there will be a special treat for Krakow people, for a very famous performer will give his puppet play, the *Szopka Krakowska*, at the Falcon Hall on Grodska Street. With him will be his wife, who will sing the hymns."

Antek put down the paper. "Our puppet show is all made."

The father: "Don't stay out too late."

Antek answered quickly: "No, little father, we won't. We will give our show several times between five and seven o'clock and then we will start on the road home."

In one corner of the little farmhouse stood a small, wooden two-towered church in miniature; between the towers at the base, large doors stood wide open, revealing a stage. And on this stage were piled a number of little wooden figures, like dolls, dressed in various jaunty colors, and in the background was the figure of a woman with a baby in her arms. This was a stage in miniature—a *Szopka Krakowska* with its little wooden puppets. When it was set up for the entertainment of lookers-on, Antek would crawl beneath it and operate the puppets from little sticks that went through a slot in the floor. This slot extended the whole length of the stage, so that a puppet could be brought upon the scene from one side, made to perform, and then be taken away on the farther side. During the performance of a puppet play the figures moved in constant succession across this stage.

The mother entered from the stove room with a huge pot of steaming soup and poured it out into wooden bowls before each of the children.

"Well, tomorrow will be Christmas Eve," she said, "and you will go out with the *Szopka*."

"Yes. And make a lot of money." This was from Stefan, the second in age. He was a more practical boy than his brother, although younger—yet he had less of the vivid imagination which made Antek the better showman of the puppet show.

The mother sighed. "I wish we could give it to you; but what we have is being laid by against the days when you go up to the university. How much did you make last year?"

"Fifty *zlotys* (about five dollars)," answered Antek proudly.

"We'll make a hundred this year," said Stefan.

"And what will you do with it?" asked the mother

A clamor went up. Antek was saying something

about a book, Stefan about a chest of tools, and Anusia, the "baby" of ten years, something that sounded like "shoes." Christopher, who played all the songs for the *Szopka* on his violin, tried to make known his want for new strings and a bow. However, the whole pandemonium was such that anyone might see that at least *something* was wanted rather eagerly. It was true, as the mother had said, that the scanty profits from the farm were going into the children's educations: Antek for the university, Stefan for the school of commerce and trade, Christopher for the academy of music, and Anusia for—well, that would come later. The child had a clear and appealing voice, and might become a great singer if placed with the proper teachers. Who knows?

Therefore this chance of making a little money on the night before Christmas meant a great deal to them all. The boys, working with the father, had built the little theater themselves. It stood upon little folding legs which Stefan had devised. The mother had dressed the dolls, and on the night before Christmas it was all in readiness to carry to Krakow. Now, since the very earliest days of the city, boys have gone about in Krakow giving this show on Christmas Eve, most of them poor or needy boys to whom the gift of money was a veritable godsend. And on Christmas Eve there descends over the earth, each year, the spirit of gladness and kindness that makes people eager and anxious to relieve suffering and soften the hard ways of life with the cheer that the Christ Child brought to men.

The day before Christmas dawned bright. It was crisp but not so cold as usual. There was not a cloud in the sky, and the children knew that they could not have selected a better day for their puppet show. At one o'clock in the afternoon they started for Krakow. Antek walked in front with the *Szopka* strapped to his shoulders. Stefan, carrying the sticks on which the *Szopka* was to rest, walked by his side. Christopher on the left side, carrying his violin and bow in a case in one hand, had extended the other hand to Anusia, who walked just beyond. A happy company it was, and all along the way people greeted them and shouted out *"Wesolych Swiat* (Merry Christmas)!" or else *"Niech bendzie pochwalony Jesus Christ* (May Jesus Christ be praised.)" As they neared the city the sun was sinking, for they had walked slowly and, too, the sun sinks early in the Christmas season. Lights were coming on everywhere, and as they stood at the Florian Gate, Anusia turning about screamed with delight and pointed at the sky.

For there, hanging like a little candle, was the first star. The Christmas season had begun.

In the market place they selected a corner by one path and mounted the puppet theater on its legs. "It was here that we stood last year," said Antek.

Candles were lighted before the little theater; a crowd gathered. Then Anusia stepped out before the people, and bravely sang a little carol, while Christopher played on the violin. The crowd increased.

"Oh, what a crowd!" cried Stefan rubbing his hands. "Here at least for the first performance is a good twenty-five *zlotys*." His words were correct. The first performance netted exactly that amount. It was a splendid performance, too: Anusia sang the carols beautifully, Antek made the puppets dance as if they were alive and everybody reached for handkerchiefs when King Herod ordered that all the babies in the kingdom should be put to death.

They had begun again when suddenly there came a rude end to their performance, and to all their hopes.

A dignitary wearing a huge star stepped into the circle before the little theater and ordered the play to be stopped.

"We can't! We can't!" shrieked Stefan, who was reading the lines for the puppets. "Don't bother us. The show must go on."

The dignitary grinned. "Where is your license?" he asked.

"License?" Antek crept out from beneath the theater where he was operating the puppets and faced the officer.

"Yes. Don't you know that you must buy a license to give public performances in this city?"

"No. It was not so last year."

"But it is so this year. It is a new ordinance that no shows may be given on the streets without a license."

"How much is the license?" asked Antek.

"One hundred *zlotys*," said the man.

"But I haven't got one hundred *zlotys*!" groaned Antek.

"Then you must move along or I will report you to the police." He motioned to a police officer on the corner.

"Come quick" ordered Antek snatching up the theater to his back. "Take the stool, Stefan, and you, Anusia, hang on to Christopher."

They emerged in a quiet place behind the Cloth Hall to take counsel.

"We can't do anything. We've got to go home," Antek announced. Every face fell. Anusia began to cry. "It can't be helped. We must obey the law and we haven't one hundred *zlotys* in the world."

"Let's give the show in some private street," suggested Stefan.

"Can't be done. We'd be arrested."

They marched out into the street. Two men engaged in a spirited conversation almost ran them down.

"Look out there," said one, sidestepping the *Szopka*. "The street doesn't belong to you boys."

"No, but we have our rights," answered Antek.

"That you have," answered the second man suddenly striking Antek in friendly fashion upon the back. "A *Szopka*, as I live!"

"A *Szopka*—" the second man fell back in amazement.

"Yes, and a good one," said the first man examining the show quickly. "Here is an answer to our prayers sent from Heaven. Do you people operate the *Szopka?*"

"We do," answered Antek wonderingly.

"Do you want an engagement?"

"Yes!" shouted Antek, Stefan and Christopher at the tops of their voices.

"Then come with us. You see, we were to have had a very famous *Szopka* with us tonight—Pan Kowalski and his wife were to entertain us. The crowd is all there—has been for half an hour—waiting for the show to begin. And there is no Pan Kowalski. We have looked up and down the town; we have hunted all

through the villages, we have inquired everywhere that
he might have been, and yet we cannot find him. We
must have the show or send the people home."

"How much do we get?" asked Stefan, character-
istically, for he had recovered from his astonishment
at this quick turn of affairs.

"We will take a collection. We can at least guarantee
you one hundred *zlotys*. You will probably make much
more than that."

As they spoke the two men hustled the children
along Grodska Street and stopped in front of a building on which there was a coat of arms bearing the
figure of a falcon.

"In here," said one of the men.

"Why this is the Falcon Hall we read of in the
newspaper," said Stefan. "This is the best place in
Krakow in which to give the *Szopka*. Antek, do you
realize"—he turned to his brother, "that we will make
lots of money out of this?"

"We must give a good performance first," admon-
ished Antek.

One of the men made a speech to the people, while
the children prepared the show. He was sorry, he said,
that Pan Kowalski had not been able to come. But in
his place there had come a very fine *Szopka* operated by
young men who were quite experienced—at this the
crowd laughed, for the youth of the performers was
quite evident. "It is Christmas Eve," the man went
on. "And it is not the time to show any displeasure.
We have come here to see acted the old story of the
wonderful evening so many centuries ago when Christ

was born to earth to bring peace and good will to all men."

It was a Christmas crowd at that, and if it felt any ill will at this substitution on the program, it did not show it. The lamp in front of the stage was lighted. Antek stepped out in front and played on his little bugle the Heynal, or little trumpet song that the trumpeter in the tower of the Church of Our Lady had played every hour of the day and night since Christianity in Krakow began. Then lights appeared in the two towers, and Christopher and Anusia stepped out to play and sing the old hymn, "Amid the Silence." The curtains were swept back by Stefan, and there on the stage were two shepherds sleeping. Red fire is burned, an angel descends, and again Christopher and Anusia step forward. This time the song is "Gloria in Excelsis," the song sung by the angels when Christ was born. The curtain is closed. It opens again on Bethlehem, whither the shepherds have come to greet the Christ Child, who lives there with the Mother, asleep on the clean hay. From the back of the manger a sheep and a cow look over the wall.

Then the scene changes. We are now in the court of Herod, the king, and Three Kings come in from the East to ask their way to the newborn king. Herod cannot tell them and so they go out again and follow a star that is gleaming in the heavens; here Stefan lifts into the air a great gold star which shines with brilliance when the light falls upon it. They come to the Christ Child and they too worship. Then the shepherds dance, and the soldiers sing, and the violin makes merry music for all the company. It is truly a splendid sight; the children shout, the babies crow and the men and women clap their hands in applause.

O thou cruel Herod! For now he commands his Hetman to send out the soldiers and destroy the Christ Child; but because they do not know who the Christ Child is, they must destroy every child in the kingdom. Cruel King Herod, for this thou shalt pay—for the floor of the stage opens and the Devil dances out; how the children scream as he cuts off Herod's head, and the head goes rolling out of the little theater and onto the floor. Then there comes more dancing and singing; little Anusia sings like an angel—the men and women take her up and the children kiss her and stroke her hands.

And when the collection is taken the bowl is heaped high with paper and silver and copper. There are at least five hundred *zlotys* upon the plate (about fifty dollars), the best day's work that any *Szopka* has ever done in Krakow. The crowd leaves slowly; the men come and take their leave of the children; the show is packed up, and the four, now beaming with happiness and delight, take again the road for the village three miles away. It is a lovely night, not over cold, but just comfortably cold, and though there is no moon, the stars are as bright as the little pinpoints of light in the *Szopka* walls. As they pass the Church of Our Lady they hear the trumpet playing the Heynal, and it makes them feel suddenly that over all the world has come this happiness at the birth of Christ.

Two hours later, on the road still, they put into the home of neighbor Kolesza for a rest. He meets them at the door with a Christmas greeting and then tells them to come to the stable for there they will find a surprise.

"I had no room for them in the house," he said. "The hay of the stable is much warmer than my floor and I have a stove here where I have heat for the animals in winter. Come and you shall see."

They entered the stable. He flashed his lantern high above his head—they looked—they drew their breaths —and then with one accord fell upon their knees.

For there in the manger was a young woman. She had been sleeping but was now awake; and in her arms, nestled close to her body, was a little baby, wrapped in a blue coat.

"It is the Christ Child," whispered Stefan. "See, there is the cow and the sheep looking over the back of the manger; and there is the place where the Wise Men knelt." He pointed—indeed a dark figure arose there and looked about; it was a man, and he put his fingers to his lips lest they should talk and disturb the mother and child.

"It is Pan Kowalski the puppet-show man," said Pan Kolesza in an undertone. "He was on his way to Krakow tonight to give a performance in the hall of the Falcons. He and his wife stopped here; and while they were here this child was born."

The children looked at one another strangely. Then they looked at Pan Kowalski, and then at the mother and the child.

"They have no money," went on Pan Kolesza; "they were to have received much money for their performance in Krakow tonight, but they were not able to go, and therefore they lose it. I do not know what they will do when they leave here, though the good

God knows I will let them stay as long as they like. They have only this show which they give at Christmas; it is not given at any other time of the year."

"And it was on this night that Christ was born. . . ." said Antek. "Stefan . . ." he added after a long pause.

"I know what you are going to say," retorted Stefan. They went out into the air again, not even taking leave of either of the men, so engrossed were they in their own thoughts.

"It means that we lose what we wanted," said Antek. "I think I'll go back."

"No," said Stefan. "Let me."

Antek squeezed something into his hand. Stefan ran back to the stable and entered. Pan Kowalski had sunk into a stupor again and heeded nothing; Stefan crept up to the manger and listened to the deep breathing of the mother. Then he slipped his hand over the edge of the manger and dropped all the silver and notes that had been collected in Krakow; then he fell upon his knees for a moment and said a little prayer. But as he staggered after his companions down the long dark road, something of the most infinite happiness seized upon his heart, and when he reached Antek he was sobbing like a baby. Whereupon Antek fell to sobbing likewise, and out there upon the Krakow road Christ was born again in the hearts of four happy children.

SECOND SERVICE OF WORSHIP

Prelude. "Heilige Nacht"

Opening Sentences

> Let Christmas not become a thing
> Merely of Merchants' trafficking,

Of tinsel, bell and holly wreath . . .
But
Let us sing unto God a new song!
For He hath done marvelous things.
Glory to God in the highest,
And on earth peace, goodwill to men.

Hymn. "Ring, O Ring, ye Christmas Bells." To the
tune, "Herald Angels")

Ring, O ring, ye Christmas bells!
Once again your music tells
Weary souls that on this morn
Christ, the friend of man, was born;
Ev'ry land, in ev'ry clime,
Hails with joy this happy time;
Gladness fills the hearts of men,
As they hear your chimes again;
Ring, O bells, your joyous lay!
All the world keeps Christmas day.

Ring, ye clanging bells, O ring!
Sing, O happy voices, sing!
Christ is born again today;
In our thought his love holds sway;
In our hearts we feel the thrill
Of his spirit of goodwill;
Once again the Christmas cheer
Brings the Master's presence near;
Thinking of his love again,
All men love their fellow-men.

Ring, ye joyous bells, O ring!
Let the earth rejoice and sing!
May the Christmas light and cheer
Light the days of all the year;
May the love that warms the heart
On this one day, set apart,

Grow until its warmth shall fill
All the earth with Christ's goodwill;
Crowning man's long quest for good
With a world-wide brotherhood. Amen.[10]

It would be well to read the verses of this hymn aloud with the group before singing it. Can we rejoice when so much of the world lies in sadness? When the very teachings of Jesus are being flouted by cruelty and war? When there is so little peace and goodwill on the earth? Let the discussion emphasize the thought that, just because of these things, we must still believe in men, as Jesus did; we must keep alive the spirit of his life; we must believe, even in the face of the present disaster, that men can learn to live together as brothers and *we* must begin, here and now, to sing our belief, to keep remembering how Jesus lived with goodwill, and to live the life of brotherhood ourselves.

Story. "The Doves of Alix" by Gertrude Crownfield [11]

Any Christmas story which stresses the religious nature of the old-world Christmas celebrations can be substituted.

At the close of the story suggest that we have taken over from other countries some of their Christmas customs. But we can be original, too. We, ourselves, can create lovely Christmas customs; in fact, we have done so. Speak of the Christmas Eve celebration on Beacon Hill, in Boston; the out-door crèche planned and carried out by the young people of one church. Or, we can take some of the old customs and put into them some new meanings. Light has, from the earliest days,

[10] By Marion Franklin Ham, *Beacon Song and Service Book.*
[11] From *The Feast of Noël*, E. P. Dutton & Company, 1928.

been a symbol to people of different races. Sometimes it has meant one thing; sometimes, another, depending upon the needs of the people. We might light the candles in our windows this Christmas Eve and, while we remember the old legends about the candle lighting the Virgin or the Christ Child wandering through the streets, as we light *our* candle this year, it might mean, "My thoughts this Christmas Eve are going out to boys and girls in Poland, in France, in Germany, in China. This is a candle of friendship, lighted in the spirit of Jesus' friendly life. I wish for the boys and girls of the world joy at this Christmas time, at least the joy of knowing that they have some friends in America. The candle will remind me not to hate anyone. May peace and goodwill come back soon to the world. And may I have a share in bringing it to pass!"

Suggest Christmas activities which individuals or groups may engage in to make this wish come true, as sending money for refugee children in our country, or to the Red Cross to make a more comfortable Christmas for children in the countries across the sea.

Prayer. Dear God, at this Christmas season, we remember, in our rejoicing, those homes in nations far away, where fear reigns instead of joy this Christmas tide. We remember those homes from which we, in America, have learned much about what Christmas really is and what it may be. As we light the candles on Christmas Eve, may we send our thoughts out across the miles to the children of France and of other countries, and wish for them a world in which there shall really be peace and goodwill. Amen.

Hymn. "O Little Town of Bethlehem"

Closing Christmas Wish (Read in unison)

A Christmas Wish

Thine own wish wish I thee in every place—
 The Christmas joy, the song, the feast, the cheer;
Thine be the light of love in every face
That looks on thee to bless thy coming year.
Thine own wish wish I thee—what dost thou crave?
 All thy dear hopes be thine, whate'er they be.
A wish fulfilled may make thee king or slave;
 I wish thee wisdom's eyes wherewith to see.[12]

THIRD SERVICE OF WORSHIP

Have a crèche set up on the altar or on a table as a focal point for this service. Keep the atmosphere informal and homelike. Recall the story of Provence, told the preceding Sunday. Talk about French children and French Christmas customs. Show some of the Nativity pictures by French artists. Imagine a French family on Christmas Eve setting up their crèche, just as many of us now do in America.

There is an old French carol which seems to say that carolers went about in the streets of French towns on Christmas Eve, singing the good news about Jesus' birth. Shall we sing it together?

Singing of Carol. "Little Children, Wake and Listen" [13]

Little children, wake and listen!
Songs are breaking o'er the earth;
While the stars in heaven glisten
Hear the news of Jesus' birth.

[12] From *Poems* by Celia Thaxter, Houghton Mifflin Company.
[13] For music, see *Beacon Song and Service Book,* No. 197; or use the tune "Austria" or "Hymn to Joy."

Long ago, to lonely meadows
Angels brought the message down;
Still each year through midnight shadows,
It is heard in every town.

What is this that they are telling,
Singing in the quiet street?
While their voices high are swelling,
What sweet words do they repeat?
"Praise to God!" The angels' chorus
Rings thro' all the earth again.
Sweetly sounds the echo o'er us,
"Peace on earth, goodwill to men."

LEADER: One of our American poets must have spent a
Christmas Eve in France once, for she has written a
poem about a French family and their crèche.

Reading of poem. "The Crèche," by Carol Ryrie Brink

Gabriel had gathered moss,
 Justine a tiny tree,
François patted out the sand
 Where Jean Baptiste could see.

They built the little stable up
 And hung the golden star;
They set the tree and spread the moss
 And viewed it from afar.

Their fingers trembled on the box
 That held the holy things;
They took the Blessed Baby out
 And dusted off the Kings.

They made a little shining pool
 From a looking glass;
François placed the shepherd lads,
 Justine the weary ass.

Joseph and heaven-blue Mary fell
    To eldest Gabriel—
The others crowded close to see
    That he placed them well.

Between these two the dimpled hands
    Of little Jean Baptiste
Laid the smiling Jesus down—
    That mightiest to the least.

When it was done they stood about
    All silent in their places,
And years and seas dissolved before
    The still light in their faces.

One said, "Joli!" and one said "Bien!"
    A radiance shown on them
As shone once on the shepherd lads
    In far-off Bethlehem.[14]

LEADER: Shall we imagine these same French children
with others all hurrying to the village church where a
larger crèche has been made and singing the carol,
"Bring a Torch, Jeanette, Isabella"? Singing of carol.
LEADER: Last Sunday we imagined ourselves on Christmas Eve crowding into a little village church in Provence and worshiping with the French peasants. Today,
the scene changes to Bulgaria.

Story. "Dobry's Christmas Crèche"[15]

"It was the day before Christmas in the little village
in Bulgaria where Dobry lived with his mother, Roda,
and his grandfather. The village was covered with snow
which had thawed and then crusted over again, but not

[14] From *The Commonweal.*
[15] From *Dobry,* copyright, 1934, by Monica Shannon. By permission of the Viking Press, Inc.

before the villagers had been able to dig tunnels out from their houses to the road. Always on Christmas Eve, Neda, Dobry's friend, and her father came to Dobry's house, because Neda had no mother. And on Christmas Eve they sat down to the simplest meal, a soup made of dried fruits, because everyone fasted forty days beforehand and did not break the fast until midnight. There was bread with the soup, a very special loaf which Roda had baked, with a very old coin baked in the middle of it. This was the gift of the Christ Child to the one who found it.

"Dark came long before they had done talking and laughing at table. 'Time to go out to the animals,' Dobry said, getting up and lighting a candle for each one to take along. For on Christmas Eve, between night and morning, every Bulgarian peasant takes up a lighted candle, goes out, wakes up each family animal and says to him or her:

" 'The Child is born and blesses you tonight.'

"Dobry had often climbed the tallest pine in his mother's forest on Christmas Eve and watched the candles all over the village going to and back from the barns and pens. But tonight his mind and spirit were both too absorbed in the dream he had mentioned to Neda—a dream alive in him, but not yet sculptured.

"For you see, Dobry wanted, more than anything else in the world, to be an artist. His mother thought he ought to stay on the farm as his father had done before him and care for the land. Dobry did not want to disappoint his mother, but always, way inside of him, was that strong wish to paint with a brush or to carve things with his hands. Grandfather had watched Dobry; he understood how strong was that wish inside of Dobry. Once or twice grandfather had talked to Roda; had said that the boy ought to be given a chance to do the thing he longed to do.

"They set off early for Christmas mass, each carrying a lighted candle.

"Their village church topped a hill and on the way up Dobry stopped climbing, and said to Neda:

" 'I like to be outside when the chimes ring, don't you? Bells sound dull, don't mean anything much when you're in the church.'

"Above them windows of the big low church lighted up, candle by candle, as altar boys hurried about inside. When all its candles burned, the village church became a Symbol of Light, a star at the top of the hill. And below Dobry and Neda the village bobbed with candles, because every peasant . . . was on his way to midnight mass.

"Husky male voices sang the Christmas canon of Saint John Damascene, greatest poet of the Eastern Church. Without an instrument of any kind, peasants stood at each side of the sanctuary's front and chanted in answer to each other, every man expressing his quickened feelings, his child-like wonder.

"And to Dobry it all seemed as old, as mysterious, as the night outside did with its symbols of God. He said no prayers in words but his mind and his heart seemed to be on fire. Longing to do perfectly what he hoped to do grew into a desire strong enough to shake him and set his blood pounding. . . .

"It was snowing when he came out of the church,

surprised to find himself alone, not realizing that the others had left before him.

"That evening they had their Christmas Eve feast and they sang around the table their favorite Christmas song:

> The Day-star of the Day-star!
> And we on earth who lay
> In death-shade and in darkness
> Have found a world of Light
> For, soothly, of a virgin
> Is born the Lord of Light.

"On Christmas morning, only Dobry in the whole village awoke early. Quietly he crept down the stairs and out to the barn where he fed the cattle, Sari and Pernik. Then he set up against a tree a charcoal sketch which he had made. He gathered together all the snow he could get in the courtyard and packed it together in a pile that stood high above his head. And then, Dobry started to fashion his dream out of snow. First he carved an open stable and after that the manger and the Holy Child and Mary and Joseph. Joseph he made to look something like Grandfather. His Mary was very much like Neda. Into his crèche he modeled his own two oxen, Sari and Pernik; and, close to the manger, he made Neda's little goat, Peter.

"Dobry told himself as an excuse for Peter's being there and nearest to the manger,

" 'The Child would love an animal, small like Peter, scraggly and with new horns. He would love it!'

"When it was done, Dobry looked at it and called it good. It was a dream he alone had dreamed and brought to life. The dream he had carried for months in his mind and heart had been born, and born alive.

"Dobry knelt in the snow but prayed for nothing. He had already emptied his mind and heart. And now without a thought to disturb him, he felt completely one with morning and snow—at peace. Without making any noise, he went upstairs again and, tired out from his work and his feeling, threw himself on the bed in all his clothes and slept.

"Grandfather went out, expecting to feed the animals and the chickens, and forgot even to question how the work had been done. He took off his sheepskin cap and knelt down before the Nativity. Too forgetful of himself for prayers of asking, he knelt there, aware only of the Holy Child who had come to their home. . . .

"Roda came out to hurry him, but instead of speaking, fell on her knees beside him. They stayed there together in complete silence, forgetful of time. The Child had come to their home. And neither of them ever before had seen a Nativity like this one. The Greek Orthodox Church has paintings but no sculpture. The Child, Mary, Joseph and the good animals blessed by the Child had been born of their snow, snow from the village sky, the water that would help create their bread and their wine.

"Roda reached out her hand to touch Grandfather. She said, 'You are right about Dobry. You are right. God made Dobry an artist and who am I to set my heart against it.'

"Tidings of the Child spread abroad and not only every peasant in the village came to visit the Holy Family, but peasants from villages miles away hitched up their buffaloes to sledges and came to pray in the snow. All day long they crowded in, and on Christmas night the courtyard was lighted by their candles and loud with their songs."

Hymn. "O Little Town of Bethlehem"

Christmas Wish. (In unison. See page 144)

FOURTH SERVICE OF WORSHIP

This service makes use of traditional English Christmas materials. Let the leader choose and arrange these materials so that they form a beautiful service of worship.

Story. The Christmas Carol by Charles Dickens

Carols

> "Good Christian Men Rejoice"
> "The First Nowell"
> "How Far Is It to Bethlehem?"

Responsive Reading

We celebrate Christmas once again. God bless it!
> Let Christmas be once more a kind, forgiving, charitable, pleasant time. May we keep our Christmas humor to the last.
The year is waning fast, and it is precious time to us. We have the power to render others happy or unhappy.
> We have the power to make their days light or burdensome, and their work a pleasure or a toil.
Our power lies in words and looks, in things so small it is impossible to add and count them up.
> The happiness we give is no small matter. We will go forth while it is day, and turn to joy the misery of men.
We will carry the torch of goodwill, that light may banish hate.

We will honor Christmas in our hearts and keep it all the year. A Merry Christmas to everyone; A Happy New Year to all the world.

God Bless us, everyone![16]

Dramatization. Six girls wearing costumes of English waits may dramatize the poem, "Six Green Singers" by Eleanor Farjeon.

For the setting for this dramatization place a high-backed chair near a table on which stands the crèche. Christmas greens may be hung over pictures or placed along the front of the platform or small Christmas trees, set in tubs, may form a background for the episode.

Let the leader explain by way of introduction that we will imagine ourselves in an old English home on Christmas Eve. The Christmas waits are caroling in the streets outside the door and the hostess is listening to them. Let the waits be in an adjoining room and let them sing one or two of the old carols. Then, let the hostess, who has been listening, say the first three lines of the poem. The waits, still outside, call, "Let us come in for Christ's sweet sake." At this point they come running in, each one carrying one of the six greens, holly, mistletoe, laurel, yew, fir and ivy. They group themselves in an informal semicircle, facing the hostess. As each speaks, she hands to the hostess her green, which the hostess, in turn, receives and places on the table near the crèche, or over the back of the chair or on the mantlepiece, depending upon the character of the setting. At the close of the poem the waits go out

[16] Adapted by W. Rupert Holloway from *The Christmas Carol* by Charles Dickens. Found in *Responsive Readings*, Iowa Unitarian Association, Beacon Press.

singing "The Holly and the Ivy" or they may remain
and lead the entire worshiping group in the singing of
English carols.

Six Green Singers [17]

(The participants are a hostess and six Christmas waits.)

HOSTESS: The frost of the moon stood over my floor
    And six green singers stood at my door.
    "What do ye here that music make?"

ALL: "Let us come in for Christ's sweet sake."

HOSTESS: "Long have ye journeyed in coming here?"

WAITS: "Our Pilgrimage was the length of the year."

HOSTESS: "Where do ye make for?" I asked of them.

WAITS: "Our Shrine is a Stable in Bethlehem."

HOSTESS: "What will ye do as ye go along?"

WAITS: "Sing to the world an ever-green song."

HOSTESS: "What will ye sing for the listening earth?"

FIRST WAIT: "One will sing of a brave-souled Mirth,

SECOND WAIT: "One of the Holiest Mystery,
    The Glory of Glories shall one song be,

THIRD WAIT: "One of the Memory of things,
    One of the Child's imaginings,

FOURTH WAIT: "One of our songs is the fadeless Faith,
    And all are of Life more mighty than
    death."

HOSTESS: "Ere ye be gone that music make,
    Give me an alms for Christ's sweet sake."

WAITS: "Six green branches we leave with you;
    See they be scattered your house-place through.

FIRST WAIT: "The staunch blithe Holly your board shall
    grace,

SECOND WAIT: "Mistletoe bless your chimney-place,

THIRD WAIT: "Laurel to crown your lighted hall,

FOURTH WAIT: "Over your bed let the Yew-bough fall,

[17] By Eleanor Farjeon, in *Come Christmas*, Frederick A. Stokes
Company, 1928.

FIFTH WAIT: "Close by the cradle the Christmas Fir,
    For elfin dreams in its branches stir,
SIXTH WAIT: "Last and loveliest, high and low,
    From ceil to floor let the Ivy go."
HOSTESS: From each glad guest I received my gift
    And then the latch of the door did lift—
HOSTESS: "Green singers, God prosper the song ye make
    As ye sing to the world for Christ's sweet sake."

ADDITIONAL WORSHIP MATERIALS

Books of Christmas Customs and Traditions

Auld, William Muir, *Christmas Traditions,* The Macmillan Company.

Coleman, Satis, *The Mystery of the Nativity in Pantomime and in Carols of Many Countries,* G. Schirmer.

Dalgliesh, Alice, *Christmas,* Charles Scribner's Sons.

Hill and Maxwell, *The Saintons Go to Bethlehem,* The Macmillan Company.

Pinkham, Eleanor, *Christmas Customs in Other Countries,* a pamphlet published by the National Council for the Prevention of War, Washington, D. C.

Sechrist, Elizabeth, *Christmas Everywhere,* Swain.

Stories Featuring Christmas in Many Lands

Alcott, Louisa, *Little Women,* Little, Brown and Company (United States).

Crownfield, Gertrude, *The Feast of Noël,* E. P. Dutton & Company (Provence).

Kelly, Eric, *The Christmas Nightingale,* The Macmillan Company (Poland).

Sawyer, Ruth, *Tono Antonio,* The Viking Press (Spain).

Seredy, Kate, *The Singing Tree,* The Viking Press, (Hungary).

Seredy, Kate, *A Tree For Peter,* The Viking Press (United States).

Shannon, Monica, *Dobry, The Viking Press* (Bulgaria).

Smith, Susan, *The Christmas Tree in the Woods,* Minton, Balch & Co. (United States).

Christmas Poetry

The Oxford Book of Christmas Carols, Oxford University Press.

Shipman, Dorothy, ed., *Stardust and Holly,* The Macmillan Company.

Slack, Elvira, *Christ in the Poetry of Today,* The Woman's Press.

Wilkinson, Marguerite, *The Yule Fire,* The Macmillan Company.

Van Loon, Hendrick W., and Castagnetta, Grace, *Christmas Carols,* Simon and Schuster.

Jesus in Art

Bailey, Albert Edward, *The Gospel in Art,* Abingdon-Cokesbury Press.

Bailey, Albert Edward, *Art and Character,* Abingdon-Cokesbury Press.

Dearmer, Percy, *Christianity and Art,* Association Press.

Eisen, Gustavus A., *The Great Chalice of Antioch,* Fahim Kouchakji, New York.

6

THE GOD OF THE UNIVERSE

"Dignity and beauty and meaning are given to our lives when we see far enough and wide enough, when we see the forces that minister to us and the natural order of which we form a part."[1]

Although young people growing up in the world of to-day have a better opportunity to understand the universe and the great cosmic forces that sustain it than boys and girls of an earlier generation, there is the possibility that they may feel less at home in this vast universe which scientists have made known than the simple peasant who has lived close to the earth and who, through necessity, has identified himself with its processes of law and mystery.

Miss Stevens says that there are two facts which pertain to every person. First, "he has been born into a universe or *unified creation*; and, he is part of a cosmic system.[2] John Burroughs has written, "Dignity and beauty and meaning are given to our lives when we see far enough and wide enough, when we see the forces that minister to us and the natural order of which we form a part."[1]

[1] John Burroughs. Source unknown.
[2] Bertha Stevens, *Child and Universe*, John Day Company, 1931, page 3.

There are several aspects of the universe which can awaken in boys and girls wonder, an emotional attitude related to the religious feelings. There is wonder at the grandeur of nature, at the regularity of natural law and at the mystery of things which are not yet explainable. In the words of Miss Stevens, "The wonder of the world should take hold of children not as miracle or magic, but as the rational succession of events uncovered increasingly by science, and leading thought on to the great How and Why which science never tries to answer. . . . What children need to become aware of is the wonderfulness of the so-called commonplaces of the natural world about them. A leaf, a stone, a star, a butterfly, a dew-drop—each one is an open book of wonder."[4]

In a world shaken with events that imperil the individual's sense of security and with boys and girls reflecting the uncertainty of the adults around them, it is possible that universe-study will do something to steady them, especially if that study is related to the great Power which sustains the universe.

> He who keeps through all his days
> Open eyes of wonder,
> Is the lord of skiey ways
> And the earth thereunder.[5]

Dr. Palmer tells of the university student who, one morning in leading a chapel service, altered the wording of the Lord's Prayer to read,

[4] *Child and Universe*, pages 10 and 11.
[5] From "Woolgathering" by Wilfred Wilson Gibson, in *Collected Poems*, Macmillan Company, 1931.

Our Father who art in the universe,
Hallowed be Thy name.
Thy will be done on earth
As it is in the universe.[6]

One of the incidental learnings which may come
through universe-study and through worship experiences which grow out of it is a certain spiritual recep-
tivity and awareness as well as a deep-seated feeling of
security, as Fannie Stearns Davis has suggested in the
following poem.

For a Child

Your friends shall be the Tall Wind,
    The River and the Tree;
The Sun that laughs and marches
    The Swallows and the Sea.

Your prayers shall be the murmur
    Of grasses in the rain;
The song of wildwood thrushes
    That makes God glad again.

And you shall run and wander,
    And you shall dream and sing
Of brave things and bright things
    Beyond the swallow's wings.

And you shall envy no man,
    Nor hurt your heart with sighs,
For I will keep you simple
    That God may make you wise.[7]

The following services and worship materials are

[6] From *The Art of Conducting Public Worship*, by Albert Palmer, The Macmillan Company, 1939, page 20.
[7] Source unknown.

designed to develop a feeling of at-homeness in the universe and to stimulate a desire for communion with the God of the universe. There are two approaches suggested. One is by way of direct experiencing of some phase of universe-study accompanied by deepening appreciation. The other is through a realization of the power and strength felt in the lives of certain people who have been keenly aware of the cosmic forces of which they are a part.

This series of services will be greatly enriched and its values will be deeper if worship grows out of some real experiencing with various manifestations of the universe. The following suggestions have to do with some of the most easily accessible materials and experiences—those which would be possible for practically any group.

SERVICES OF WORSHIP

FIRST SERVICE OF WORSHIP

Let us begin with some informal approaches to worship.

1. Conversation about sunsets, stars, moon, eclipses. If any have seen a total or partial eclipse of the sun, encourage them to tell how it made them feel. Be sure that all understand what an eclipse is. Do any of them know any constellations by name? Have any ever watched one star every evening over a period of time? If not, perhaps they would like to begin to do so and note its position in the sky each successive evening.[8]

2. Examination of the globe and of the planescope.

[8] For further suggestions, see *Beginnings of Earth and Sky*, by Sophia L. Fahs, Beacon Press, Teachers' Manual, 1937.

Talk about the sun, its light, the distance it travels; the moon as reflecting the sun's light; other stars with their suns; a universe full of stellar systems; the size of the earth compared to other stars and planets.

3. Ask members of the group to tell about wonderful sunsets which they have seen. What made them wonderful? Color? Cloud effects? The after-glow? Has anyone ever watched a sunrise? Did you notice the difference in that the radiant glow in the sky follows the setting sun, but flushes the sky in the early morning before the sun rises over the horizon?

4. What does the surface of the moon look like? What are the dark spots on the moon's surface, which look to us like the man-in-the-moon or the lady-in-the-moon? Mountains, plains, seas. Note that the moon differs from other satellites in that no other known satellite is so large in proportion to the planet which it attends.

There are certain parts of the sky where we see great groups of stars together. These are sometimes called star cities. The Milky Way is one of these which most of us have seen easily. On clear nights it seems quite near us with its millions of stars twinkling away. But actually, all those stars in the Milky Way are so far away from us that the light from them takes fifty thousand years to reach us. That is, the light we see, when we look up, started to come to us fifty thousand years ago.

5. Picture and poetry appreciation. Show the picture, "When I Behold Thy Heavens," by W. L. Taylor. Sometimes when we first look up at the heavens at night we are able to see only a few stars. Then, after we have

looked for a long time, we begin to see other stars in the depth of the blue. Let us look at the picture quietly while the piano plays some music about the evening star. Perhaps, as we look, we shall seem to see the stars coming out and then disappearing and reappearing again.

As the pianist finishes playing Wagner's theme, "To the Evening Star," the leader may begin to read quietly Sara Teasdale's poem, "Stars."

> Alone in the night
> On a dark hill
> With pines around me
> Spicy and still,
>
> And a heaven full of stars
> Over my head,
> White and topaz
> And misty red;
>
> Myriads with beating
> Hearts of fire
> That aeons
> Cannot vex or tire;
>
> Up the dome of heaven
> Like a great hill,
> I watch them marching
> Stately and still,
>
> And I know that I
> Am honored to be
> Witness
> Of so much majesty.[9]

Ever since the world began men have looked up at the

[9] From *Flame and Shadow*, The Macmillan Company.

starry heavens and have been filled with wonder. The Hebrew shepherds on the hills of Palestine, watching their sheep at night, looked up at the stars and felt much as this modern poet has felt. One of these early Hebrews voiced his feelings in one of our Psalms.

> The heavens proclaim God's splendor,
>   the sky speaks of his handiwork.
> When I consider the heavens, the work of thy fingers,
> The moon and the stars which thou hast ordained,
> What is man that thou art mindful of him?
> And the son of man, that thou visitest him?
> O Lord, how manifold are thy works!
> In wisdom hast thou made them all,
> The earth is full of thy riches.

SECOND SERVICE OF WORSHIP

The materials on the browsing table may be related to the theme of this series of worship services on "The God of the Universe." If possible have available pictures of an eclipse. If a picture of an eclipse can be thrown on the screen as the group assembles for worship, it can become a worship center while the prelude is being played. Books of nature poetry may be consulted by the boys and girls during the pre-session period.

Prelude. "Largo," by Handel (For interpretation of this selection, see page 182)

Call to Worship

> God of grave nights,
> God of brave mornings,

God of silent noon,
Hear my salutation.[10]

Hymn. (Sung to the tune "Salve Domine" or "Lancashire")

God of the busy daytime,
God of the quiet night,
Whose peace pervades the darkness,
And greets us with the light,
Safe with thy presence near us,
Wherever we may be,
Thou God, our great Protector,
We love and worship thee.[11]

LEADER: Some of you have been looking through our poetry books to find some poems about the moon or the stars or other wonderful things in God's world. Do you want to read them to us now?

Poems. (Read by volunteers)

The following are suggested as types of poems which might be found in books on the browsing table:

"The Night Will Never Stay," by Eleanor Farjeon[12]

"The Procession," by Margaret Widdemer[12]

Conversation. Pupils may tell about some wonderful things they have seen. This informal conversation may be omitted if the leader thinks best.

Story Material

In the year 1933, on the thirty-first day of August,

[10] From "A Chant Out of Doors" by Marguerite Wilkinson, in *Blue Stones*, The Macmillan Company.

[11] By Thomas R. Birks, from *Hymnal for American Youth*, H. A. Smith, Ed., D. Appleton-Century Company, 1928.

[12] Found in *Two Hundred Best Poems for Boys and Girls*, Whitman Publishing Company, 1938.

at a certain hour in the afternoon, the earth in certain places became dark, as though it were night. This was the moment for which scientists had been waiting and watching for a number of years. Hundreds of thousands of years ago, when this strange thing happened, men were probably very much frightened and thought the sun god was angry with mortals. Later on, when they still did not understand, some thought that the end of the world was at hand. But today, men know all about this strange event; they knew it was coming; they knew the exact moment at which to expect it. There were just certain places on our earth's surface where this strange thing could be seen and astronomers from all over the world had gathered at these places to study the heavens and to take photographs. So far have men been able to discover God's laws since those earliest times that they could plan to a second just when the total eclipse of the sun would occur.

Other people, besides astronomers, traveled great distances to see the eclipse. On mountain tops, along country roads, beside the ocean they gathered, and suddenly through darkened glass they saw the very beginning of the moon's body start moving across the sun. Little by little it crept along until half the sun was covered. By this time the light was beginning to grow dim, like a late winter afternoon. Slowly, on crept the shadow across the sun until only a slender disk of light was left. People held their breaths as the world grew darker and darker; flowers began to fold their petals, as they do when night comes on. Then, in another moment, the last ray of light was blotted out and those who were watching could see the wonderful corona (or crown) of light around the dark spot where the sun was hiding. Only once in a great many years does the moon pass between the earth and the sun, but men can tell to a second just when this will be, so sure are the laws by which our universe is run.

To be able to foretell an event like this with such certainty seems more wonderful when we think of how far away from us the moon and sun and stars are, and how many millions of star worlds there are in the universe. When we look up at the sky on a clear night, it sometimes seems studded with stars. Without any telescope, just with our eyes we can see three thousand stars. That would be about as many as there are letters in all the words on two pages of an ordinary book. But to really imagine the total number of stars in the sky we must think of a huge library of at least a half-million books. All of the letters in all of the words in all of these books would just about equal the number of stars which are in the sky.

Yet, on any evening, if we step outside our homes and look up into the heavens, we can know exactly where to find certain stars. We can know beforehand, by looking at our calendar, on just what night the moon will be full, so surely and so regularly do these millions of heavenly bodies move through the universe.

Scripture. Psalm 8

LEADER: Sometimes we feel very small indeed when we think of God's boundless universe full of many worlds, some much bigger than our earth, each one revolving through space in perfect order, some of them sending their light to us millions of miles away. But, though we sometimes feel very small, we are also thrilled with wonder when we think that man, with his brain for thinking things out, has been able to discover many things about these worlds in God's universe. When Galileo made his telescope, it seemed like magic. But how little he could see through it compared with what men can see today at one of our great observatories! Today men have discovered a photographic process by which they can actually take pictures of stars that are so far away no one can see them even through the most powerful telescope. When we think of these things, we feel, as did the psalmist, that "man is only a little lower than the angels" and we are glad that we can share some of God's thoughts with Him and that we can discover some of His laws. Once the astronomer, Kepler, after he had been looking up into the distant heavens, exclaimed, "I think thy thoughts after thee, O God."

As the Hebrew psalmist wrote in poetry how the stars made him feel, a poet of today has written a poem that tells how we feel when we look up into the heavens.

> A little star creeps o'er the hill,
> While woods are dark and birds are still;
> The people fold their hands in prayer,
> And the love of God is everywhere.[13]

A Moment of Silence. In which we think about how we can count on God's laws and the wonder of a universe full of worlds, all running according to law.

Hymn. "God of the Earth, the Sky, the Sea," Samuel Longfellow

[13] See page 186 for music. The word "people" has been substituted for "children."

THIRD SERVICE OF WORSHIP

Prelude. "Largo," by Handel

Call to Worship

LEADER:
>   Stand still,
>   think of the wonders of God,
>   When God works, do you know how?——
>   how he makes lightning flash from the clouds?
>   Do you know how the clouds are poised,
>   that pour a deluge when it thunders?

UNISON RESPONSE:
>   This is the doing of the Eternal——
>   we can but watch and wonder.[14]

Hymn. "God of the Earth, the Sky, the Sea"

Hymn Appreciation

LEADER: Joseph Haydn was born into a very poor home. The house was a little one with a thatched roof. Haydn's father did iron work and made wheels and carriages and worked hard at his trade. But, while he worked, he sang. He loved to sing. He did not know a note of music, but he could play the harp and so he played and sang in the evenings and the neighbors came in to listen.

One night when Joseph was six years old, a cousin was visiting them and during the music-making he heard little Joseph sing. "He has a beautiful voice," said this cousin, who was the choir director in a near-by town. So, he persuaded Haydn's parents to let the little

[14] From *The Moffat Bible: A New Translation* by James Moffat, Harper & Brothers.

boy of six go with him and join his choir. This cousin taught Joseph music and the boy never again lived at home. He sang regularly at the church services and came to love the beautiful music that made people think of God. When he was eight a great choirmaster from the big city of Vienna heard him sing and asked to take him away with him to join his choir.

But Joseph Haydn went through a great many hard things before he became famous. When he was eighteen, his voice left him and he was dismissed from the choir. Suddenly he found himself with no home to turn to (his parents had both died), no friends on whom he could call for help, nothing to wear except the clothes on his back and nothing to eat. On the first night after his dismissal from the choir he slept out of doors on a bench. It was a cold November night. In the morning he met an old friend who lived in a very poor house. But he told Joseph that he could come and live in his garret.

The years passed by and Joseph Haydn kept on studying and writing music until he made himself known. And through all the years he felt often that God was speaking a message through the music he wrote. One of his greatest compositions is called "The Creation." It tells about the wonders of the universe which God has created. Haydn said, "Never was I so religious as when I was composing 'The Creation.' I knelt down every day, and prayed to God to strengthen me for my work." When he was very old, just before he died, he was taken to hear a performance of his own great music, "The Creation." As he entered the music hall, which was crowded with people, he was greeted by a burst of trumpets and great applause. When the chorus sang the song, "And there was light," the applause of the audience was terrific, but Haydn would not let the people praise him for making such beautiful music. He exclaimed, pointing up, "It came from there." One of our hymns is set to a part of Haydn's "Creation" music. The words, written by Addison, tell of the stars and the moon and the entire heavens shouting the glad news that God made this wonderful world in which we live.

Hymn. "The Spacious Firmament on High"

Glorious Things of Thee are Spoken #80

> The spacious firmament on high,
> With all the blue ethereal sky,
> And spangled Heav'ns, a shining frame,
> Their great Original proclaim.
> Th'unwearied sun from day to day
> Does his Creater's pow'r display,
> And publishes to ev'ry land
> The work of an almighty hand.
>
> Soon as the evening shades prevail
> The moon takes up the wondrous tale,
> And nightly to the list'ning earth
> Repeats the story of her birth;
> Whilst all the stars that round her burn,
> And all the planets in their turn,
> Confirm the tidings as they roll,
> And spread the truth from pole to pole.

LEADER. Of all the good tidings men have wanted to hear, nothing has so comforted them and given them courage as to feel sure that God is in His world and is always near them.

Scientists have discovered laws of the universe and have said, "God must be behind these laws."

Artists have seen beauty and have said, "Only God can make the earth so beautiful."

Musicians have heard sounds which other ears could not hear and have composed great music. And the people, listening to that music, have said, "Only God could help man put together sounds to make such music."

Prayer. O God, as we look at the world you have made; as we see the stars come nightly to the sky; it is as though the stars and the sun and the planets were all trying to say to us, "The hand that made us is God's." We are glad you are a living God and that there is so much in the world to remind us of you. We are glad, this morning, for music that tells the good news that God is in the universe. Amen.

LEADER: Years ago the Hebrew psalmist, looking up at the night sky in Palestine, felt the same way as Addison and Haydn did when they wrote this song of creation.

Psalm 19

> The heavens proclaim God's splendor,
>   the sky speaks of his handiwork;
> day after day takes up the tale,
>   night after night makes him known;
> their speech has never a word,
>   not a sound for the ear,
> and yet their message spreads
>   the wide world over,
> their meaning carries to earth's end.[15]

An Act of Wonder

> Our wondering questions pierce the skies.
> How long back to the first beginning?

[15] From *The Moffat Bible: A New Translation.*

How far off to the farthest star?
Who can tell what the smallest things are?
How are the stars in their courses bound?
Is there a place where God is found?

It takes more than angels to hold the stars high,
It takes more than minds to know God by.
We question the earth,
We question the stars,
We question the best that in us lies;
We question also if evil dies.

Messages come surely to listening ears,
They may take a hundred
Or a thousand years.
Our children may hear them,
Or their children's children.
With each answer we know
Our wonderings grow.[16]

Quiet Music. "How Beautiful upon the Mountains,"
Handel

FOURTH SERVICE OF WORSHIP

Prelude. Selections from "The Creation," Haydn

Hymn. "The Spacious Firmament on High"

Call to Prayer

A little thing is our earth,
Slung, by a thread unseen,
In a tiny trail round a lesser star;
Beyond it——Infinitude,
Universe beyond universe,
Bright, estranged, unknowable.

. . . .

[16] From *Beginnings of Earth and Sky*, by Sophia L. Fahs, Beacon Press, 1937, pages 153-154.

A little thing is our earth
And beyond it is Infinitude.[17]

Silence
Prayer

God of grave nights,
God of brave mornings,
God of silent noon,
Hear my salutation!

Silence
An Act of Praise

O Lord, we praise thee for our Brother Sun,
Who brings us day, who brings us golden light;
He tells us of thy beauty, Holy One.
We praise thee, too, when falls the quiet night,
For Sister Moon and every silver star
That thou hast set in heaven clear and far.

For our brave Brother Wind we give thee praise;
For clouds and stormy skies, for gentle air;
And for our Sister Water, cool and fair,
Who does us service in sweet, humble ways;
But when the winter darkens, bitter cold,
We praise thee every night and all day long

For our good friend, so merry and so bold,
Dear Brother Fire, beautiful and strong;
For our good Mother Earth, we praise thee, Lord;
For the bright flowers she scatters everywhere;
For all the fruit and grain her fields afford;
For her great beauty and her tireless care.[18]

[17] From *Sacraments of Common Life* by J. S. Hoyland, W. Heffers and Sons, Ltd., Cambridge, 1927, page 23.

[18] From *God's Troubadour*, Sophie Jewett, Thomas Y. Crowell Company, 1910.

A Psalm of God's Glory. (See under "Scripture," page 188)

An Act of Wonder. (See previous service)

Hymn. "O God Our Help in Ages Past"

FIFTH SERVICE OF WORSHIP

Prelude. "Communion," Edward Batiste

Call to Worship

LEADER:

Think of the wind, fresh and strong, carrying the leaves so lightly. We cannot see the wind; yet it touches us.

Jesus said:

"The wind blows where it wills; you hear its voice; but you cannot tell from whence it comes or where it goes. So is God's spirit."

God is Spirit.

We cannot see the wind; but the wind is here.

We cannot see God.

But He is here.[19]

RESPONSE:

We do not see the wind,
   We only hear it sigh;
It makes the grasses bend
   Whenever it goes by.
We do not see God's love,
   But in our hearts we know
He watches over us
   Wherever we may go.[20]

—ELIZABETH CUSHING TAYLOR

[19] From *Children's Praises* by N. Simpson and L. E. Cox, Student Christian Movement Press, London, 1934, page 56.

[20] From *Picture Story Paper*, Board of Education, Methodist Church. Used by permission of the author.

Hymn. "Joyful, Joyful, We Adore Thee," Beethoven

Story

Louisa could have shouted for happiness. But she decided she had better keep her shouts until she got out of doors. She stood in the middle of her very own room, the first room of her own she had ever had. She was thirteen years old and it seemed to her she had been waiting for this moment all her life.

Life looked very exciting. The Alcott family had just moved two days before and they all loved their new home. It was such a funny old house with about seventeen doors in it. Whenever a neighbor knocked, the whole family went scampering in every direction, for no one could tell on which one of the seventeen doors the neighbor had knocked.

There was a stairway which wound up and up, from the very first floor to the top of the house where one came out onto a flat place and could look out all over the surrounding country. It would be a great place to play their favorite game "Pilgrim's Progress," thought Louisa. What fun it would be when their bundles dropped off and went bumpty-bumping down two flights of stairs to the bottom!

As for the barn, it was the very place in which to stage their plays. Louisa was already writing a new one, called "The Witch's Curse." It was going to be thrilling.

As Louisa stood there in the middle of her room that spring morning, she could have hugged herself for joy. Over by the window was her little desk, where she planned to write a great many stories and plays. She puckered up her nose and sniffed in the delicious odor of dried herbs which Marmee had hung in her closet. And there was the door which opened right from her room out into the garden and onto the hillside which rose directly in back of the house. Louisa looked out up that hillside and thought, "I can run off to the woods whenever I like."

You see, one reason Louisa was so happy to be in the new home was because she felt that a new life was beginning for the whole family. The last few years had not been very happy ones. Their father and some friends of his had got the idea that they ought to live away off from other people and not eat anything or wear anything that caused any harm to men or beasts. So the family had moved out to a place called Fruit-lands, where a lot of people came to live with them and they could wear linen clothes and no leather shoes and they could only eat fruits and dried vegetables and a few things like that. Poor Marmee had to work so hard cooking meals for all these people who had come to live with them and sitting up late at night doing the mending. This made Louisa angry—to see her beloved Marmee working so hard. So Louisa rose at five every morning, had her bath in icy-cold water, carried wood for the fire, washed the dishes and even did the iron-ing. Louisa and her sisters had to sleep in the attic, there were so many people living in the house with them, and some nights when Louisa went up to her bed under the eaves in the attic she was so tired she cried a little bit. All the time they were at Fruitlands the Alcotts were very poor.

On this spring morning, Louisa was singing to her-self, "But things are going to be better; things are going to be different!" That night she wrote in her diary:

"March, 1846. I have at last got the little room I have wanted so long and am very happy about it. It does me good to be alone, and mother has made it very pretty and neat for me. . . .

"I have made a plan for my life. I have not told anyone about my plan but I am going to be *good*. I've made so many resolutions. . . . Now I'm going *to work really* for I feel a real desire to improve, and be a help and comfort, not a care and sorrow to my dear mother." [21]

The summer passed—such a happy summer. There were plays in the barn to which all the Concord children were invited. There were long hikes through the woods with their kind friend, Mr. Thoreau, who told them all about birds and trees and flowers. They held strawberry parties in the rustic arbor on the hillside back of the house. And whenever Louisa wanted to, she could go off by herself and be alone in her pretty room. There were times when she liked to be alone with her thoughts. One night she kept waking up to watch the moon shining through her window and she wrote in her diary the next day, "I had a pleasant time with my mind, for it was happy."

And whenever she felt like it, Louisa could open the door of her room, the door that opened out into the garden, slip out quietly and run to her heart's content through the woods along the hilltop.

One beautiful October morning when the maples

[21] From *Louisa May Alcott, Her Life, Letters and Journals,* Ednah D. Cheney, Ed., Little, Brown and Company, 1930, page 36.

were scarlet and yellow, before anyone else was awake, Louisa opened this outside door and slipped out into the autumn sunshine. She stood for a moment breathing in the crisp October air. Then up to her beloved woods she raced. And while she was up there in the woods something wonderful happened to her. It was so wonderful that in the evening, sitting at the little desk in her own room, she wrote about it in her diary. This is what she says:

"Concord, Thursday. I had an early run in the woods before the dew was off the grass. The moss was like velvet and as I ran under the arches of yellow and red leaves, I sang for joy, my heart was so bright and the world so beautiful. I stopped at the end of the walk and saw the sunshine out over the 'Virginia Meadows.'

"It seemed like going through a dark life or a grave into heaven beyond. A very strange and solemn feeling came over me as I stood there, with no sound but the rustle of the pines, no one near me, and the sun so glorious, as for me alone. It seemed as if I *felt* God as I never did before and I prayed in my heart that I might keep that happy sense of nearness all my life."[22]

The years passed by. Miss Alcott had written *Little Women* and *Little Men* and had become famous for her stories. One day she got out this diary which she had written when she was a little girl. When she got to this part of her journal, she wrote in the margin:

(I have kept this happy sense of nearness all my life.) [23]

[22] *Ibid.*, pages 33-34.
[23] *Ibid.*

LEADER:

Louisa's father and mother often talked to her and her sisters about "growing" stronger and better and braver and kinder. Let us pray a prayer for growingness.

Prayer:

> We praise Thee, O Lord, for all growing things:
> Leaves on tree and hedgerow, blossoms in our gardens.
> Grant that we too may grow
> Stronger and taller,
> Happier and more kind,
> Loving Thee more and more every day. Amen.[24]

Hymn. "God Who Touchest Earth with Beauty" (To the tune "Geneva" or "Bullinger")

> God who touchest earth with beauty,
>   Make me lovely too,
> With thy Spirit re-create me,
>   Make my heart anew.
>
> Like thy springs and running waters,
>   Make me crystal pure,
> Like thy rocks of towering grandeur
>   Make me strong and sure.
>
> Like thy dancing waves in sunlight,
>   Make me glad and free,
> Like the straightness of the pine trees,
>   Let me upright be.
>
> God, who touchest earth with beauty,
>   Make me lovely too,
> Keep me ever, by thy spirit,
>   Pure and strong and true.[25]

[24] From *Children's Praises*, by N. Simpson and L. E. Cox, Student Christian Movement Press, London, 1934, page 101.

[25] By Mary S. Edgar. Used by permission of the International Council of Religious Education and of the author.

A service in which we express our appreciation of those who have helped to discover some of God's laws.

This service will have meaning for the boys and girls if they have some of the stories of the different explorers, especially in the field of the physical sciences. Emphasis can be given to the fact that even scientists today do not know all the answers to all the questions that we and they would like to have answered. But through the years there have been some, like Galileo, Copernicus, Madame Curie and others, who were the first to discover some of God's laws which govern the many worlds in his universe. Some of these people were so far ahead of their day that they were laughed at and some of them suffered hardships and even death. But God's laws seemed so wonderful to them and they were so eager to find out all they could for the service of mankind that they kept right on with their explorations. Materials such as the following might be used in this service. Other scientists could be added or substituted, depending upon which ones are most familiar to the group.

Discoverers of God's Laws

FIRST PUPIL: The astronomer, Kepler, studied the stars and exclaimed, "I think thy thoughts after thee, O God."
SECOND PUPIL: Sir Isaac Newton made such wonderful discoveries about light that an English poet, Alexander Pope, wrote about him:

> Nature and Nature's laws lay hid in night;
> God said, "Let Newton be," and all was light.

THIRD PUPIL: In Westminster Abbey where England's great men are honored, there is a statue of James Watt, with these words below it:

James Watt

· · · · · ·

Enlarged the Resources of His Country
Increased the Power of Man
and Rose to an Eminent Place
Among the Most Illustrious Followers of Science
And the Real Benefactors of the World

FOURTH PUPIL: Sir Humphrey Davy, after discovering how to make a lamp which miners could wear without danger of explosion, was urged by a friend to patent his idea and make money on it. To this he replied, "My sole object was to serve humanity, and if I have succeeded I am amply rewarded. I have never received so much pleasure from any other of my chemical labors, for I trust the cause of humanity will gain something from it."

FIFTH PUPIL: Madame Curie, who, with her husband, discovered radium, refused to make money on it. She said, "We are working for science. Radium is an element. It belongs to all people."

SIXTH PUPIL: Albert Einstein, the greatest of modern scientists to discover the laws of God's world, has also devoted his life to outlawing war and bringing peace among the nations.

Unison Reading. Evidences of Faith in Modern Achievement

By faith Marconi reached out into the air and sent the messages of mankind around the world, thus drawing all mankind into a unity of thought which makes for world friendship.

By faith Alexander Bell, in long, weary hours of study and work, achieved the telephone, linking towns, states and continents into a fellowship of work and pleasure through the extended sound of the human voice.

By faith Edison, taking the spark of power generated in the worship of God, gave to our homes light and power for the comfort and efficiency of our daily lives.

What more shall we say of our great men of science, who seek out the uncharted paths of discovery; delving deep into the mysteries of the laws of the Creator; thinking God's thoughts after him, enduring many hardships and great dangers that they may make known his wonders through faith?

By faith they conquer the elements, discover the treasures of the earth and increase the power of man until he is indeed but a little lower than God.

By faith these men have entrusted us with vast power and limitless strength in the use of their great inventions.

Wherefore, seeing that we are surrounded by so great a cloud of witnesses, let us dedicate ourselves to using all these inventions and our great power to the service of man. Let us vow not to destroy life but to build it up and make the world a world of beauty and of peace.[26]

[26] Adapted from a selection by Laura Armstrong and a group of high-school students, found in *The New Hymnal for American Youth*, H. Augustine Smith, Ed., D. Appleton-Century Company, 1928, page 332.

Prayer. (In unison)

O God, who has made so many worlds, we boys and girls living on one of thy worlds are filled with wonder when we think of thy greatness. We feel the power of the lives of these brave men and women who have explored thy laws and made them known to us. We feel that it is wonderful to be alive in this age when any day some discoverer may find out something new about our universe. Since we live in so wonderful a world, help us to live lives that are great and unselfish. Some of us, when we are older, may be explorers like the men and women whose lives we have come to admire. But all of us can keep thy laws and work with thee to make this world a better place for all people to live in. May we remember that the greatest people have used power to build up and not to destroy. Amen.

Hymn. "These Things Shall Be, A Loftier Race," John Addington Symonds.

Additional Worship Materials

Stories.

1. A story to develop appreciation of Handel's "Largo."

Many years ago when our country was just being settled by English and French colonists, there was born across the seas in a little German town a boy by the name of George Friederich Handel. George Friederich might have had a very happy childhood except for one thing. For the one thing he most wanted in all the world his father would not let him have. Now this one thing was to be allowed to make music.

George Friederich's father had made up his mind

that George Friederich was not to know anything about music. His father was determined that the boy should become a lawyer and grow wealthy and well known. So his father said he never wanted to hear George Friederich play upon any kind of an instrument.

But there was someone (we do not know who) who felt that it was a terrible crime to keep this gifted little boy from learning to play. This unknown friend probably said to himself or herself, "If George Friederich can learn to play, some day he will make music that will make the whole world happy." So this friend smuggled into the house, when the father did not know it, a clavichord. This was a tiny piano with the keys fixed so that they made no sound. Up to the dim, dark attic the little clavichord was carried. In the night, long after everyone had gone to bed, little George Friederich would steal, oh, so quietly, out of his room, close the door softly and climb up to the attic. There, by the flickering light of a candle, he played on the keys and taught himself music.

One day when George was about seven years old, his father was going by stagecoach on a journey to the palace of a duke. George Friederich begged to go.

They went to the duke's chapel where a service was going on. George Friederich almost trembled with happiness when he heard rolling through the stone arches of the chapel the tones of the organ. After the service the boy somehow slipped up into the organ loft and suddenly through the air came floating the tones of the organ. It was not the organist playing. Who could it be?

The duke and George Friederich's father and the organist all went to see. And there he sat, such a little boy, making such beautiful music. Of course the secret was out now. The father heard about the practicing in the attic and the duke heard how the father had forbidden the boy to learn music. The duke talked to George Friederich's father and made him see that George ought to be taught music. So, when they returned home, George was sent to a great organist who taught him, not only to play, but to compose music as well. His teacher had the choir sing George Friederich's music and often the boy took his teacher's place at the organ at the Sunday services.

One of the pieces of music which he composed is called the "Largo." People in every country of the world have loved to listen to it, for its great chords seem to make them feel the greatness of this universe which God has created.

2. "Sir Isaac Newton's Story," from *Beginnings of Earth and Sky* by Sophia L. Fahs.

Explain in connection with this story that the words of the hymn, "The Spacious Firmament on High," were written by Joseph Addison who lived after Sir Isaac Newton had told the world some of his thoughts about the laws of the universe. The hymn, "O God Our Help in Ages Past," was also written by a man who lived after Newton's discoveries.

Scripture to accompany this story might be selections from Psalm 104 in the translation by Moffat.

3. The story of Copernicus. From the following story outline the leader may create his own story. With some of the suggested source materials at the close of this chapter he may build a service of worship.

STORY OUTLINE

a. The boy Copernicus, always studying, first in

Poland, then in Italy. Studied law, medicine, natural science, mathematics.

b. A young man of many interests. A skillful painter, interested in civics; translated books from the Greek.

c. His greatest interest was astronomy.

d. A growing conviction that the earth moved in its circuit once a day.

e. Ridicule of people, who said: a) if the earth moved, its motion would be felt; b) if the earth moved and you jumped, it would whiz by you before you could land; c) a moving earth would fly to pieces.

f. Copernicus worked until he proved that the sun is the center of the universe and all other planets move around it, including the earth. He also showed how vast is the universe. People were astonished at the things he said about the worlds.

g. People demanded proof of these things and Copernicus could not prove them, because there were no telescopes strong enough to see these worlds so far away.

h. Copernicus never saw the wonder in the eyes of the people when his theory was proved. That was left for another man later. He began to write his ideas in a book.

i. Copernicus was taken ill and just before he died the first copy of·his book was placed in his hands As he held the book in his hands, he knew that, though the people did not believe him then, the time would come when they would understand that he was right.

Music

1.

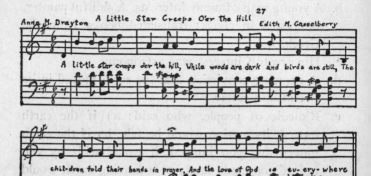

A Little Star Creeps O'er the Hill

Anna M. Drayton

Edith M. Casselberry

A lit-tle star creeps o'er the hill, While woods are dark and birds are still, The chil-dren fold their hands in prayer, And the love of God is ev-ery-where

2. A poem by the American poet, John Greenleaf Whittier. The music for this can be found in many hymnals.

> I know not what the future hath
> Of marvel or surprise,
> Assured alone that life and death
> His mercy underlies.
>
> I know not where his islands lift
> Their fronded palms in air;
>   I only know I cannot drift
> Beyond his love and care.

3. Song Response

> Lord of the sunlight,
> Lord of the starlight,
> Lord of the seasons,
> Teach me to know

[27] From *Primary Music and Worship*, Presbyterian Board of Christian Education, 1930, page 71.

How best to love thee,
How best to serve thee,
Mid summer's flowers or winter's
    snow.[28]

4. Hymn, "God of the Glorious Sunshine"

God of the glorious sunshine,
God of refreshing rain,
Whose voice bids earth awaken
And clothe itself again.
With life of richest beauty
In plant, in flower, and tree;
Thou God of light and splendor,
We rise and worship thee.

God of the hill and mountain,
Of valley and of dale,
Whose finger paints the rainbows;
Thy beauties never fail
To raise our souls in wonder,
And turn our thoughts to thee;
Thou God of living nature
We stand and worship thee.

God of the busy daytime,
God of the quiet night,
Whose peace pervades the darkness
And greets us with the light,
Safe with thy presence near us,
Wherever we may be,
Thou God, our great Protector,
We love and worship thee.

God of the whole creation,
God of all life below,

[28] From *Songs For Little People*, Pilgrim Press. Used by permission of the author, Isabel Fiske Conant.

We seek thy nearer presence,
Thy grander life to know;
When we, thy heightened splendor,
Thy greater glories see,
Thou God of all creation,
We still shall worship thee. Amen.[29]

5. Other hymns to use in this series.

"All Creatures of Our God and King," by St. Francis

"For the Beauty of the Earth"

"O God Our Help in Ages Past"

"All Beautiful the March of Days"

Scripture. The Heavens Declare the Glory of God

O Lord, our God,

How wonderful Thou art in the whole earth!

When I look up into Thy heavens; and see the moon and
the stars which Thou hast made

And know that some of those little stars are other whole
worlds and are many times larger than our world,

I think how small men and women and boys and girls seem!

Yet Thou hast made them with hearts that love and minds
that think;

They are almost like Thee and Thou dost love them.

Thou hast let them rule over Thy great universe which
they are learning to understand.

Thy children have learned to use many of Thy glorious
gifts.

They have learned about the animals and use them for
food; birds and fishes also they can know.

Even the stars in heaven are charted by them.

O Lord, our Lord, how wonderful Thou art to us! (Psalm
8:1, 3-9)[30]

While the earth remaineth, seed time and harvest, and cold

---

[29] From *New Hymnal for American Youth*, H. Augustine Smith,
Ed., D. Appleton-Century Company, 1928.

[30] This arrangement is found in *Thoughts of God for Boys and
Girls*, Connecticut Council of Churches.

and heat, and summer and winter, and day and night shall
not cease. (Genesis 8:22)

Poetry.

1. "Going to School to God," by William L. Stidger

I like to go to school to God!
  I hear such strange revealing things;
He talks to me where rivers run
  And where a skylark soars and sings.

He teaches me his love and care
  Through every tree and blade of grass
Here on the hill, where I may sit
  And listen while the wild winds pass.

He writes with glaciers on the rocks
  And with the stars that blaze on high;
With fossil shells and ferns that fall
  And leave their imprint as they die.

His books are beds of slate and coal;
  His manuscripts sequoia trees;
While earthquakes punctuate the tale
  And turn the pages of the seas.

His blackboard is a canyon wall
  Whereon he writes of ages past.
In even lines the strata tell
  Of things that shall forever last.

He writes with rivers, and they carve
  The crevices he leaves, to tell
The story of his living love
  In temple, tower and pinnacle.

I like to go to school to God!
  Because it always seems to me

He talks in every breeze that blows;
    Through every bud and bird and tree.[31]

2. "Lovely Is Thy Universe," by Keith Thomas

How infinitely tall are Thy skies, O Lord!
The wings of men's minds grow weary; still rise
In vastness beyond them Thy skies.

The mighty winds blow and the stars wheel
In the enormity of Thy space;
The great sun sets and the shadows steal
Across the smallness of the earth's face.

Night grows and the darkness around us,
Yet we are not afraid while the earth runs
Its course, for we know Thou hast found us
And comforted us and called us Thy sons.

Lovely is Thy universe, O Lord;
Teach us to be unafraid of the vastness that lies
About us, and above us in Thy skies.[32]

3. For other poems see the following:
   a. Barrows, Marjorie, Ed., *Two Hundred Best
      Poems for Boys and Girls*, Whitman Publish-
      ing Company.

     "Planting a Tree," by Nancy Byrd Turner
     "Velvet Shoes," by Elinor Wylie
     "The Night Will Never Stay," by Eleanor
      Farjeon
     "Silver," by Walter de la Mare
     "The Procession," by Margaret Widdemer

[31] From *I Saw God Wash the World*, by William L. Stidger, Rodeheaver-Hall-Mack Co., Chicago, 1934, page 14.

[32] From *Poems for Life*, Thomas Curtis Clark, Ed., Willett, Clark & Company, 1941.

"Stopping by Woods on a Snowy Evening,"
by Robert Frost

b. Thompson, Blanche Jennings, Ed., *Silver Pennies*, The Macmillan Company.
c. Huffard, Carlisle and Ferris, *My Poetry Book*, John C. Winston Company.

Prose Selections

A Conservationist's Creed

Stop killing and start creating. Stop cutting and start planting. Stop wasting and start saving. Stop hunting and start watching. Stop hating and start loving. These are the ten commandments of conservation for each of us within his own dooryard and neighborhood, over his own ranch and farm, a sower of seeds, a planter of trees, a nourisher of life, where heretofore we have each plucked and buried and slaughtered.[33]

—Dallas Lore Sharp

Prayers

1. Prayer in the Woods

Trees towering majestically overhead, reaching up their
arms to God;
Clouds floating lazily along in the blue sky;
The forest floor, carpeted with ferns and wild flowers;
Birds singing joyous songs of praise;
Butterflies flitting through the air;
And me, standing all alone with an awed feeling,
Before the works of God.[34]

2. A Prayer of Wonder

O God, how many are Thy works!

[33] Used by permission.
[34] By a junior high school girl, from *A Summer Book for the Family*, Connecticut Council of Churches and Religious Education.

In wisdom Thou has made them all.
For all wonderful things,
>The ones we know,
>The ones that are secrets waiting for us still,
We praise Thee, O God! Amen.[35]

Pictures

"When I Behold Thy Heavens," by W. L. Taylor, Curtis Publishing Company. Now sold in small and large copies by Edward Gross Co., 118 E. 16th Street, New York.

Pictures of the Eclipse, *National Geographic Magazine*, issues of the year 1933.

Stevens, Bertha, *How Miracles Abound* and *Child and Universe*. Beautiful photographs of familiar things in nature, showing nature's observance of the laws of symmetry and design.

[35] From *Children's Praises*, by Simpson and Cox, Student Christian Movement Press, London, 1934, page 131.

INDEX

of First Lines of Poems, Prose Selections and Prayers

193

Index of Titles of Poems, Prose Selections and Prayers

Index of Stories and Dramatizations

(Except in cases where other authors are mentioned the stories are written by *Marie Cole Powell*)

Index of Authors